1999

CAMBRIDGE CONCISE HISTORIES

A Concise History of South Africa

This book provides a succinct synthesis of South African history from the introduction of agriculture about 1,500 years ago up to and including the government of Nelson Mandela. Stressing economic, social, cultural and environmental matters as well as political history, it shows how South Africa has become a single country. On the one hand it lays emphasis on the country's African heritage, and shows how this continues to influence social structures, ways of thought and ideas of governance. On the other, it chronicles the processes of colonial conquest and of economic development and unification stemming from the industrial revolution which began at the end of the nineteenth century. This leads on to a description and analysis of the fundamental political changes which South Africa is currently undergoing, while providing a background for the understanding of those many things which have not changed.

ROBERT ROSS, a lecturer in history at Rijksuniversiteit Leiden for the past twenty years, has published widely on South African history. His most notable books are *Adam Kok's Griquas* (1976); *Cape of Torments: Slavery and Resistance in South Africa* (1982); *Beyond the Pale: Essays in the History of Colonial South Africa* (1992); and *Status and Respectability in the Cape Colony, 1750–1870* (1999).

CAMBRIDGE CONCISE HISTORIES

This is a new series of illustrated 'concise histories' of selected individual countries, intended both as university and college textbooks and as general historical introductions for general readers, travellers and members of the business community.

First titles in the series:

A Concise History of Germany
MARY FULBROOK

A Concise History of Greece
RICHARD CLOGG

A Concise History of France
ROGER PRICE

A Concise History of Britain, 1707–1975
W. A. SPECK

A Concise History of Portugal
DAVID BIRMINGHAM

A Concise History of Italy
CHRISTOPHER DUGGAN

Other titles are in preparation

A Concise History
of South Africa

ROBERT ROSS

CAMBRIDGE
UNIVERSITY PRESS

PUBLISHED BY THE PRESS SYNDICATE OF THE UNIVERSITY OF CAMBRIDGE
The Pitt Building, Trumpington Street, Cambridge CB2 1RP, United Kingdom

CAMBRIDGE UNIVERSITY PRESS
The Edinburgh Building, Cambridge CB2 2RU, UK   http://www.cup.cam.ac.uk
40 West 20th Street, New York, NY 10011-4211, USA   http://www.cup.org
10 Stamford Road, Oakleigh, Melbourne 3166, Australia

First published 1999

Printed in the United Kingdom at the University Press, Cambridge

Typeset in 10/13 Montype Sabon in QuarkXPress™   [SE]

A catalogue record for this book is available from the British Library

Library of Congress Cataloguing in Publication data
Ross, Robert, 1949 July 26– .
A concise history of South Africa / Robert Ross.
p. cm.
Includes bibliographical references (p. 202) and index.
ISBN 0 521 57313 0. – ISBN 0 521 57578 8 (pbk).
1. South Africa – History.   I. Title.
DT1787.R67   1999
968–dc21   98–11691 CIP

ISBN 0 521 57313 0 hardback
ISBN 0 521 57578 8 paperback

PULA!

and in celebration of the release
of Nelson Mandela from gaol and its consequences

CONTENTS

ILLUSTRATIONS

MAPS

ILLUSTRATION CREDITS

Natal Museum: 1.1.
South African Library, Cape Town: 1.2; 2.8.
Angas, *The Kaffirs illustrated*: 1.3.
Isaacs, *Travels and Adventure*: 2.2.
Schapera: 1.4.
Moffat, *Missionary Scenes and Labours*: 1.5.
Rijksmuseum, Amsterdam, collection Jan Brandes: 2.1.
MuseuMAfricA, Johannesburg: 2.3, 2.5, 2.7, 2.9, 3.2, 3.7, 3.8.
Thompson, *Survival in two worlds*: 2.4.
Preller, *Voortrekkermense*: 2.6.
University of the Witwatersrand, Johannesburg: 3.1, 3.5, 4.1, 4.4, 5.3.
Bailey's historical archive, Johannesburg: 5.2, 6.4, 6.4.
Brandt, *Zuid-Afrika*: 3.3, 4.3.
Rhodes Centenary Exhibition, Bulawayo, *Catalogue*: 3.6
Our First Half-Century, 1910–1960, Golden Jubilee of the Union of South Africa: 4.2.2., 5.1.
Sandberg, *Twintig Jaren*: 3.9.
Hancock, *Smuts*: 4.2.1.
Illustrated London News (Courtesy of the Koninklijke Bibliotheek, Den Haag): 3.4.
Malan, *Afrikaner Volkseenheid*: 4.2.3.
Sundkler, *Bantu prophets*: 4.8.
Nederlands Instituut voor Zuidelijke Afrika: 4.6, 4.7, 6.2, 6.3, 7.1, 7.4.3.
Pieter Boersma: 7.4.2, 7.5.
Jan Stegeman: 7.4.4.
Cape Times: 6.1.
Iafrica:, 7.2, 7.3, 7.7.4, 7.8, 7.9.
Nederduits gereformeerde kerk, Cape Town: 7.4.1.
Vilakazi, *Zulu horizons*: 7.7.1.
Feesalbum, Suid-Afrikaanse Academie vir Wetenskap en kuns: 7.7.2.
Mayibuye Centre, University of the Western Cape: 5.4, 7.7.3.
The Star, Johannesburg, 7.10, 8.1.

PREFACE

This book was written during my tenure of a fellowship at the Netherlands Institute for Advanced Study, Wassenaar, during the Academic Year 1996–7. I would like to thank the Institute for the support and conviviality it gave, and also the Faculty of Arts of Leiden University, my employer, for allowing me leave of absence. I would also like to thank Dmitri van der Bersselaar, Jan-Bart Gewald, Janneke Jansen, Adam Kuper and Barbara Oomen for their critical comments on various of the chapters.

TERMINOLOGY AND
ORTHOGRAPHY

Terminology and orthography are the bugbears of South African historians, as they are often highly contested signs. I have done my best to render personal names in the orthography used by the individual concerned or his or her descendants. The prefixes of words in Bantu languages have been added for ordinary nouns, and for ethnonyms and their derivatives. Thus Sesotho is the language of the Basotho (singular Mosotho), who live in Lesotho, isiZulu that of the amaZulu in KwaZulu and so forth. (The apparently eccentric capitalisation is that of current orthographies.) Where I have used these as adjectives, I have not provided prefixes, which would of course depend on the class of the noun so modified. Thus I write of the Tswana people, but of the Batswana. Place names are generally the modern ones, thus Maputo for Lorenço Marques. I have used the names of the post-1994 provinces where appropriate to designate geographical areas, but where the area I wish to describe is included in several modern provinces, I have not hesitated to use older appellations. Thus I write of Mpumalanga rather than the Eastern Transvaal, but of the Southern Transvaal to refer to an area now included in the provinces of Gauteng, part of Mpumalanga and part of the North-West Province. I have also written of the Transkei and the Ciskei to describe the regions in question, although the Bantustans with these names have thankfully disappeared. The names were of course older than the Bantustans. The titles of certain acts of legislation have been retrospectively changed to accord with modern sensibilities. Thus the Natives Land Act of 1913 is now generally known as the Black Land Act. I have tended to maintain the original description, out of a dislike of anachronism. I appreciate that the names were somewhat insulting (though there were many worse), but so were the acts.

The various African languages all have their own orthographies, which are not consistent with each other, nor even between the Sesotho of Lesotho and that of the Republic. Four points need to be made. First, in isiXhosa and isiZulu, the letters 'c', 'q' and 'x' refer to the dental, palatal and lateral clicks peculiar to these languages (though the palatal is also to be found in Sesotho) and above all to the Khoisan languages (where they have specific signs). The unskilled should pronounce them all as 'k'. Secondly, the sound of 'ch' as in the Scottish 'loch' is written 'g' in Setswana and other languages, but as 'x' in some Sesotho variants and as 'r' in isiXhosa. Thirdly, Lesotho Sesotho has an orthography derived from the French, in which in particular an 'o' before another vowel is pronounced as 'w'; thus the repeated syllable in 'Moshoeshoe' is pronounced, *mutatis mutandis*, rather like the drink firm Schweppes. Fourthly, 'h's generally signal the aspiration of the previous consonant, to demonstrate a phonemic difference most Europeans do not hear, although it is essentially that of the old distinction in English, now only heard in the mouths of Scottish speakers, between 'where' and 'wear'. This however is not the case with 'sh', as in 'Shaka' or 'Moshoeshoe', which is pronounced as in English.

Introduction

South Africa is a single country. At one level this may seem to be an extremely banal statement, but at another it is highly contested. For many years, the Government of the country denied it. Even now, South Africans have to struggle to recognise it. The African National Congress, which sees itself as the embodiment of the nation's unity, campaigned under the slogan: 'One Nation, Many Cultures'. Archbishop Desmond Tutu writes of 'The Rainbow People of God'. The country has eleven recognised official languages. The divisions within it are so great that to call it single is thought of more as a programmatic statement, a pious hope, than as a statement of fact.

The view from the outside, where this book is written, is different. After all, all countries are divided by the cultural background ('race' or 'ethnicity') of their citizens, by religion, by economic differentials, by gender. In South Africa, these splits may be sharper than elsewhere, but they are not of other kinds. Indeed, however much they may emphasise the distinctions between themselves, South Africans are immediately recognisable as such, no matter where in the country, socially and geographically, they originate.

This book is an attempt to show how South Africa became a single, though not uniform, country. That it has become so should not be a matter for dispute. Take, for instance, the country's economy. Throughout the twentieth century, and indeed beginning much earlier, there has been a steady incorporation of previously more or less independent units into a single interdependent totality. There can now not be any household in the country which is not tied in all sorts of ways into the national (and thus the international) economy. South Africa no longer has any exclusively subsistence peasants. Culturally, no process of homogenisation has taken place. South African society is probably as diverse, possibly more diverse, than ever. Nevertheless, the cultures that have developed are only local when, as is the case with certain of South Africa's ethnicities, they have been created in almost conscious rejection of values which, within the confines of South Africa, are universal. Far more generally, the developing cultural forms, for instance as expressed in religion or in music, are only in inessentials geographically limited. Certainly, people in all the major urban centres, in differing proportions, find the same sorts of ways of understanding and giving meaning to the chaos of their lives. In the countryside, too, the experience of a century of migrant labour has drastically affected the ways in which society is organised and the values that are held. There are uniformities across the country in this, and also many influences from the towns where, after all, many country dwellers spend much of their lives. Politically, the domination of the central state, which has steadily increased ever since Union (1910), has created a single arena in which the various conceptions of how South African society should be ordered compete. The long exclusion of the great majority of South Africa's adult population from formal participation in the political life of the country in fact only accelerated the general realisation that local conflicts were played out according to rules set by the central government, and thus formed part of country-wide political disputes. And, of course, the events of the 1990s have conclusively demonstrated the sham that always was the Balkanisation of the country through the creation of Bantustans. Anyway, these were always proof of the great reach of central Government.

Beyond this, though, what matters is the sort of country that South Africa has become, and is still becoming. Indeed the rate of social and political change is now greater than ever before. Nevertheless, South Africans of the last decade of the twentieth century are having to work within, and to cope with, the heritage of their past, recent and distant. In very broad terms, that past has created a country with the following characteristics. It is an African country, and the social structures and, just as important, modes of thought of pre-colonial African societies continue to shape its present. Modern family structures and ideas about governance and the reasons for misfortune, for instance, still owe much to a pre-colonial past. It is an ex-colonial country. Its very shape is that determined by the limits of colonial conquest at the end of the nine-teenth century. Indeed, uniquely, it has been at once a colony of white settlement, a colony of slave labour and a colony of rule over a large autochthonous population. In this sense, it was a colonial country plus. It is a capitalist country, or at least a country whose economic develop-ment has been dominated by capitalist organisations. Colonial South Africa was founded by the premier capitalist corporation of the seven-teenth century, the Dutch East India Company, and was taken over by the British at the height of Britain's industrial revolution. Later, South Africa was transformed, from the last quarter of the nineteenth century, as a result of the discovery and, more importantly, the exploitation of its massive mineral deposits, notably of diamonds and gold. The par-ticular forms of labour organisation that these mines developed did much to shape the social structure of the country, and on their back sec-ondary industry and the tertiary sector have developed to a degree unexceeded on the African continent. In consequence of this, it is an urban, or at least an urbanising, country. By 1996, about 55 per cent of South Africa's population lived in towns. However, the policies of apartheid had kept the proportion of urban Africans relatively low, at two-fifths of the African population. With the abolition of the laws that kept many of the Africans in the countryside, this percentage is increas-ing rapidly. Finally, South Africa is a Christian country, though not exclusively. Approximately three-quarters of all South Africans now claim to be members of a Christian church, either of a world-wide denomination or of one of those many which have been created in South Africa itself.

These various strands in the country's history are of course not inde-pendent one of the other. It is out of their interweaving that modern South Africa has been created. It is my purpose in this book to explicate their interconnections and development.

Yet, even if the essential unity of South Africa and the identity of South Africans are beyond dispute, there remains the question of what is, and what is not, South Africa. Who are, and who are not, South Africans. Historically, these matters are by no means clear. Until 1910, there was no such entity as South Africa, except as a geographical expression. Before then, for instance, Moshoeshoe, the founder of the modern independent kingdom of Lesotho, was as much a South African as his contemporary Sekhukhune, whose descendants are now chiefs in the Northern Province of the Republic. After 1910, at various times, the South African government attempted to incorporate Namibia, which is now an independent country, and to divest itself of large areas of its territory, the Bantustans, together with perhaps half its population, which are now again integral parts of the country. Many of the labourers in the country's gold mines have always come from outside the formal borders of South Africa. At times, and for some subjects, it makes sense to write about South Africa in the narrowest sense, that of the modern Republic, or indeed that which was under the rule of the colonial governments and their successors. At others, the focus needs to be on the whole region, including at least Botswana, Lesotho, Swaziland, Namibia and southern Mozambique as well as the Republic. I hope that it will be clear from the context what at any given moment I mean by South Africa, and why, but, even more than is the case for most countries, the definition of what is South Africa is, in practice, remarkably fuzzy.

I

The settlement of the country

South Africa is at once an old and a new country, and was so long before the New South Africa was called into existence in the 1990s with the balance of the Old unredressed. It is old geologically. Only in the far north-west, and in a few isolated pockets, is the land covered by recent deposits, producing the highly permeable, and thus dry, sands of the Kalahari, which indeed cover most of Botswana and much of Namibia. Elsewhere the ancient rocks of Gondwanaland come to the surface. In the southern two-thirds of the country these are mainly the sedimentary rocks of the Karoo series, but in the north they are Pre-Cambrian or older, often interlaced with igneous irruptions and thus blessed with one of the world's widest assemblages of minerals.

The rocks have weathered to produce a land surface dominated by a plateau 1,500 to 2,000 metres above sea level. This is surrounded by a roughly semi-circular escarpment, which is only broken by two rivers, the Gariep (to give the Khoi name, now taken back into use, for the river generally known as the Orange) which flows into the Atlantic and the Limpopo which forms much of the country's northern border before flowing through Mozambique to the Indian Ocean. Neither they nor any of the shorter rivers which flow off the escarpment, and are longest in the south of the country, are navigable. The mountains of the escarpment are highest in the east, where they form the Drakensberg chain. These break the rain-bearing weather systems which come in off the Indian Ocean in the summer. As a result the narrow strip between the sea and the mountains in the south-east is well watered and was once largely covered with woodland or forests. In the rest of the

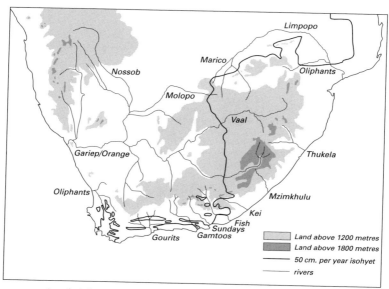

1 South Africa: physical

country the thick savanna of the far north thinned out to grassland on
what became known as the High Veld and, further south and west, to
the semi-desert of the Karoo and the Kalahari. Only in the far south-
west of the country is the pattern different. There, the climate is similar
to that of the Mediterranean or California as rain systems come in off
the Atlantic in the winter. Also, there is a small stretch of the southern
coastal belt which receives rain throughout the year and is thus
forested.

The country is also old in terms of human habitation. Many of the
fossils of humanity's ancestors have been found in South Africa, as have
some of the earliest remains of men and women of the modern type.
Over the millennia, these people lived by collecting roots, nuts and other
plant food, by gathering shellfish on the coast, by fishing and by hunting
the abundant antelope and other game. They fashioned the landscape
with fire, and may indeed have created the grasslands of the High Veld
in this way, but were not otherwise intrusive into the environment. The
first domestication of South Africa only began a couple of thousand
years ago, with the introduction into the sub-continent of herding and
agriculture. Relatively speaking, this was late. Southern Africa was

probably the last major region of the Old World where this development occurred, at least before the ecologically disastrous efforts to irrigate the central Asian steppe in the present century.

In the course of this development pastoralism preceded agriculture by some centuries. At some stage in the last half of the first millennium BC, people living in the region where modern Botswana, Zambia and Angola meet acquired sheep and, possibly later, cattle, and began to move south into the highlands of central Namibia and into the High Veld and the Cape. Like their predecessors in the region, they spoke a language containing many clicks, a phonetic feature unique to Southern (and Eastern) Africa, but it was different to those languages used south of the Kalahari up till then. This began the process whereby language became a marker for way of life which has characterised Southern Africa ever since. This process was accentuated after the introduction of agriculture south of the Limpopo river in the first half of the first millennium AD. For as long as there is information, and probably since their arrival, up to the coming of European colonists, Southern Africa's agriculturalists – who should properly be described as agro-pastoralists, since cattle were very important in their economies, and more so in the underpinning of their social structures – have spoken one of the closely related Bantu languages. These form a branch of the Niger-Congo family which is the major language group in Africa, with derivatives spoken from Senegal to the Cape. Indeed, the relatively recent settlement of South Africa by speakers of these languages can be gauged from their close linguistic relationship and from the fact that the two major variants, Nguni (including isiXhosa, isiZulu, siSwati, which were all spoken between the escarpment and the Indian Ocean, and isiNdebele) and Sotho-Tswana, spoken largely on the interior plateau, which within the group are more or less inter-intelligible, are both found over a very wide area. In addition Tshivenda, closely related to languages across the Limpopo in Zimbabwe, is spoken in the far north and what was to become crystalised as Xitsonga was and is to be found in the north-east of the country, as well as across the border into Mozambique.

In the course of the first millennium, then, there developed in Southern Africa a tripartite division of the population. There were the hunter-gatherers, later known collectively as 'Bushmen' or 'San', speaking one of the Khoisan 'click' languages, the pastoralists, speaking Khoikhoi, also Khoisan, and the agriculturalists, who spoke one of the

Bantu languages. The boundaries between the groups were never impermeable. In economic terms, all groups hunted and collected wild plant food, though very few Bantu-speakers fished or collected shellfish. All Bantu-speaking groups owned cattle, and indeed the Ovaherero of central Namibia were almost exclusively pastoralist, though they, like certain Khoisan, grew a number of crops, particularly dagga, the South African version of marijuana. IsiXhosa, isiZulu and, to a lesser extent, Sesotho accepted clicks into their phonetic repertoire, and physical anthropological studies have shown that considerable numbers of Khoisan at least were incorporated into the Bantu-speakers, whose ancestors, migrating from further north, were typically darker in appearance than the Khoisan. However, since people who changed life-styles also changed languages, the divisions appeared much firmer than they actually were, and where they lived in the same area contacts between the groups were continual.

As, over the centuries, the sub-continent came to be fully settled, the agro-pastoralists came to dominate all those areas which were ecologically suitable for their way of life, that is to say roughly the eastern half of modern South Africa, the eastern fringe of Botswana and the north of Namibia. Further west, not enough rain fell to sustain agriculture, or, as in the far south-west, fell at the wrong time of the year for the crops they grew. The Khoikhoi lived mainly along the well-watered southern plains, and also along the Gariep river and in the highlands of the western escarpment both south and, especially, north of the river. The Bushmen were increasingly a remnant population, living in contact with the others but in areas where agriculture and pastoralism were unattractive or too risky, particularly in the mountains of the Drakensberg and the Western Cape and in the semi-deserts of the Karoo and the Kalahari.

The various Bushman groups had a variety of cultural elements in common. They all lived in relatively small bands, which came together around a source of food and water when these were plentiful, and dispersed across the countryside in seasons of scarcity. Equally, a common cosmology was spread across a wide area and was expressed both in mythology and other forms of oral literature and in visual art, painted onto the walls of the shelters in which they lived or inscribed on rock platforms and pebbles. The oldest such art has been dated to 27,000 years ago, but most is much more recent, and was being produced into

1.1 This rock-painting, depicting eland, was removed from the farm The Meads in southern Natal to the Natal Museum to prevent further water damage.

the nineteenth century. Primarily it is figurative, representing humans, animals and figures which are at once human and beast and are thought to represent the trance experience of Bushman shamans. While most of the game available to the Bushmen was painted somewhere, there is a heavy over-representation of certain species, notably the eland which occupied a central place in Bushman mythology. While the engravings are generally line drawings, and many of the paintings are effectively monochrome silhouettes, a number, notably in the Drakensberg, are in shaded polychrome. Together, they comprise the highest concentration of the genre anywhere in the world, and aesthetically they represent one of the high points of human visual creativity, with an importance which stretches far beyond the bounds of Southern Africa.

Khoikhoi social organisation differed from that of the San largely as a result of the greater size of political unit that herding made possible. Among the Bushmen, every member of the group was thought of as a relative and addressed as such; among the Khoikhoi this was not possible, and far greater stress was laid on relationships in the male line. Conversely, Bushman life did not allow for the accumulation of property; the lucky and skilful Khoikhoi herder could acquire a substantial number of cattle and sheep, which he could both pass on to his sons and use to bind others to him as his clients. Such individuals became political leaders. Khoikhoi society was thus literally plutocratic. A ruler's authority derived from his wealth, and disappeared if that wealth was dissipated or captured by enemies. Nevertheless, in normal times such authority, and thus the tribal groupings, were relatively stable, both along the southern coast and in Namaqualand and Namibia. Its fragility would only be evident after the advent of European colonialism.

Both pastoralism and agriculture were introduced into Southern Africa. A few plants – various melons, some greens, rooibos tea for instance – have been domesticated in the region, but these do not form the staples on which people rely. Crops were brought into the region at most a century or two later than cattle and sheep, but their spread was much slower. The mixed farming regime, often known as agro-pastoralism, entailed the steady subjugation of the landscape, but for the first few centuries of such settlement the farmers, naturally enough, concentrated in and on the deep soils of river valleys in KwaZulu-Natal and what used to be the Transvaal. Here they grew sorghum and bulrush and finger millets, together with pumpkins, melons and no doubt sundry garden vegetables. Their stock was probably not abundant, except in the far north and in north-east Botswana substantial herds were built up, sufficient to degrade the environment and cause a crisis for the societies based on pastoralism by about 1250 AD.

By this stage, virtually all the eastern half of South Africa had been colonised by the agro-pastoralists, as had northern Namibia, where the cultural traditions were rather different (and thus not included in this account.) In so doing, they had turned the bush into agricultural land, thus restricting the tsetse fly, which carries the parasites for sleeping sickness in humans and a more deadly cattle disease, to a narrow zone along the Limpopo. The agro-pastoralists' material culture, particularly their housing, which can be reconstructed by archaeological research, was already broadly similar to that described in detail from the early nineteenth century onwards. Since the lay-out of homesteads was determined by an underlying symbolic system which, with variations, was constant over space and over time, it is reasonable to assume that the other main features of their social organisation were also in place at least five hundred years ago.

1.2 Khoikhoi family group, with their stock, as drawn by an
anonymous Dutch artist around 1700.

These features included, first, a sharp division of labour between the sexes. Essentially, two separate spheres of production obtained. Women were thought to be dangerous to cattle, and were excluded from pastoral activities, and thus implicitly from political power. They performed the bulk of agricultural labour. While men were responsible for clearing the fields of trees, something that had to be done most years as fertility was quickly lost and plots were not kept in use for long, it was the woman's task to prepare the soil by hoeing, to plant, to weed (often accompanied by her daughters), to harvest and to thresh the grain. While the crops were growing young children would be employed scaring off the birds. Women also collected wild food in the *veld*, fetched water, gathered firewood or cow dung for cooking and prepared the thick porridge which was the staple food and the beer, and washed the utensils after meals. The timber or stone work for the building of houses was done by the men, and in some parts of the country they did the thatching. Women, on the other hand, plastered the houses, on the walls and floor, with cow dung, built the lower retaining walls around the homestead, and generally kept the homestead clean. Potting, and in some places basketry, were also within the women's realm.

The adult men, in contrast, were primarily concerned with the livestock. They may not actually have engaged in herding to any great extent; in times of peace this was the task of the boys, who were first assigned to the small stock and later, when around ten years old, to the cattle. Milking the cows, thickening and souring the milk into *amasi*, butchering animals and working the leather produced from their skins were in principle men's work. Men would also build the cattle byres, with poles and brushwood. Other male tasks included smithing, for a small, specialised group, mining, particularly for copper in the far north and near the border with Mozambique (iron was far more widely available) and war, public affairs and politics.

The two spheres were linked to each other through the institution of bridewealth (*bogadi* in Sesotho and Setswana, *lobola* in the Nguni languages). This was the key institution around which the societies of the region were organised, at the level of the family. A woman moved from the family in which she was born to that of her new husband, where she would labour in the fields, cook, keep house and, hopefully, give birth to children. In return for this loss of labour and reproductive potential, her husband, aided by his family, would transfer cattle to his wife's

1.3 This painting, made in the 1840s, shows a homestead near modern Umlazi, in KwaZulu-Natal. Occupied by a polygamous family, it is well away from other settlements in the area. This was generally the case in the well-watered lands between the Drakensberg and the Indian Ocean, where homesteads were scattered fairly evenly across the ridges of the hilly countryside.

father and brothers, in part at once, in part only when she had demonstrated her fertility by having a child. From then on she was a member of her husband's family, even if he died. In such circumstances, one of his brothers would take her over, but any children she had would nevertheless be considered the legal heirs of the dead man. Divorce was possible, but rare, since in general the bridewealth had to be returned. This was obviously not wanted by her male relatives, who were the main people who could offer her sanctuary, particularly as the bridewealth cattle had often been used to obtain a wife for one of her brothers. The pressure on her to remain with her husband was therefore very great. If a woman was abused too excessively, she might return to her own family, which after a court case might possibly retain the bridewealth they had received. All the same, this did not usually happen.

Family membership was essentially patrilineal, that is to say only those related to each other exclusively through male links would be thought of as part of the group. A man would look on his brother's son, for instance, as part of his own family, his sister's son as closely related, but not part of the same family. Among the amaNguni, men and women from the same family could not marry, and indeed a king could split the royal family by marrying one of his distant patrilineal relatives, thereby excluding his new wife's close kin from the succession. Elsewhere, it was often thought preferable that a man should marry a woman to whom he was closely related, particularly one of his cousins. If these marriages were repeated over the generations, the bridewealth cattle would be seen as returning to the family they had left, and in time the edges of the family group would become less clear.

This system was predicated, not perhaps necessarily but certainly in fact, on the subordination of women to men (and to a lesser, because impermanent, extent of young men to their elders). Women's work was physically harder, and more continuous, than that of the men. Marriage was seen as the alliance between two families, and women had relatively little say in the choice of partner. Among the amaNguni, a wife was expected to show respect for her new family by employing elaborate circumlocutions so as not to pronounce the names of her male in-laws. She was also not allowed to drink the milk of her family's herds until she had had a child. As she herself grew old, and became a mother-in-law, or even the mother of the homestead head, the sharpness of the oppression could decrease, but she remained juridically subservient to men, even indeed to her own son. Moreover, if she were to prove to be barren, her life would be very hard. Her family would be expected to provide a sister or niece to perform her reproductive tasks, and she herself might be cast off into poverty as her ability to labour diminished.

Children were brought up in such a way that the gender norms were inculcated from a very young age. From the age of about six, girls were expected to help their mother around the homestead, learning from her how to prepare food and to work in the fields. They would also have to fetch water and firewood. Boys in contrast would at the same age be assigned the task of looking after the stock, first sheep and then, later, cattle. There they would grow up under the tutelage of somewhat older youths, forming gangs and learning to fight, initially with sticks. Those from prominent families would also accompany their fathers to public meetings, and thus acquire an education in government.

When they reached puberty, both sexes underwent initiation to allow them to reach full adulthood. Again the initiation schools were segregated by sex. The girls received instruction in the skills required for being a good wife. The boys completed their training as future warriors. Those who were initiated together acquired an *esprit de corps* and, under the leadership of a chief's son or some other high-born youth, would form a fighting unit, usually known as a regiment.

Viewed from the perspective of men, the system allowed the possibility of accumulating people and, hence, power. Since land was fairly freely available, and private property in land did not exist, and since the level of technology was such that it was difficult to distinguish oneself from one's fellow on the basis of the possession of physical objects, what mattered was the acquisition of cattle and dependents. It was here that the bridewealth system had political connotations. The number of wives that a man could have was in the first place dependent on the size of his cattle herd, and thus on the number of women for whom he could pay bridewealth. Furthermore, a man with many wives was able to offer much hospitality, above all in the form of beer, and thus to increase the respect in which he was held by his peers.

The chiefs could follow these strategies with greater success than commoners. The non-Khoisan population of pre-colonial South Africa all lived under monarchical systems of government, presumably according to ideas of the proper ordering of society which had been brought with the immigrants from further north in the first half of the first millennium AD. At times, the major state systems which had developed on the Zimbabwe plateau spread out to include the Limpopo valley and adjacent areas of the Northern Province and Botswana. The well-known archaeological site at Mapungubwe, close to where the modern countries of Botswana, Zimbabwe and South Africa meet, was the capital of such a state. In general, though, at least until the mid-eighteenth century, the political units under which South Africans lived were small, particularly in KwaZulu-Natal and Mpumalanga. In the Eastern Cape and on the High Veld, in contrast, the kingdoms were often large enough to allow a certain degree of hierarchy among the various chiefs, so that a ruler would have had more office-holders subordinate to him.

In material terms, chiefly power was based on the accumulation of cattle and people. These might have come to him through successful war. For instance, Moshoeshoe of Lesotho acquired both his great

1.4 Part of the Kgatla capital of Mochudi in modern Botswana, in the 1930s. On the High Veld and in the Kalahari margins, the rulers attempted to concentrate their subjects in large towns, directly under their supervision. During the summer, people dispersed across the countryside, to cultivate their fields, but during the dry season, the largest of these towns would have a population in excess of 10,000 people.

initial herds and the name by which he was known – it is onomatopoeic, meaning the 'shearer' – as the result of a successful raid. In addition, the bridewealth system was worked to their advantage. Presumably because of the benefits seen to derive from connections by marriage with the chiefly family, a chief had to pay less bridewealth for a wife than did a commoner, and would receive much more on the marriage of one of his daughters. The bridewealth for his chief wife, who would be the daughter of another chiefly family, was even paid by his followers. In consequence, there was a steady syphoning of people and cattle upwards to the chiefly families. In the mid-nineteenth century well over half of Xhosa cattle were owned by the aristocracy, and by the mid-twentieth a seventh of the population of Swaziland carried the royal family name, Dlamini. Chiefly cattle would be dispersed among the commoners, both for the sake of security, and because the recipients, who would receive recompense for their care of the beasts in the form of a proportion of the calves born, would be further tied to chiefly authority through relations of patronage.

Chiefs had to foster such relations because ultimately the power of an individual ruler was contingent on his performance. Not every man could become a chief. In principle the office was hereditary, and even in the most turbulent times a leader had to have, or to claim, patrilineal descent from the chiefly families. Individual men, or groups of them, were often not rigorously tied to a particular chief. Inertia, loyalties and practicalities would make it a major decision to leave one chief for another, but if his government failed, individuals and groups would do so, attempting to take as many of their cattle as possible with them. This often happened after a disputed succession, when the loser would remove himself with his supporters, or when an eldest son, who had built up power during his father's lifetime, had to make way for a younger half-brother, who was the son of an aristocratic chief wife, but there could also be a steady drift from an unpopular or unsuccessful ruler. As the Batswana put it: *Kgosi ke kgosi ka batho* – a chief is a chief by the people, and thus, conversely, a chief without people was no chief. People claimed their political identity from the chief to whom they were, perhaps only temporarily, subject. To give an example, by the name by which they call themselves, the amaSwati express their allegiance to the successors of Mswati, a king who ruled in the mid-nineteenth century. (The modern country goes under its isiZulu appellation since 't's in siSwati are pronounced as 'z' in isiZulu.) Political units, later called 'tribes', were thus contingent on the flow of events, and were not permanent entities. A successful ruler would have people of many backgrounds among his followers.

This expressed the ultimately consensual nature of chiefship. West of the Drakensberg, this was given concrete expression in what the Batswana called the *kgotla* (*kgôrô* in Sesotho). These were, and are, at once gatherings of all adult men (in recent times women have also been allowed to attend and to speak) living in each individual ward, a section of a town or stretch of countryside, or of the polity as a whole, and the open space where such gatherings take place. East of the escarpment, these meetings are known as *izindaba*. The *kgotla* or *indaba* functions as a court of law, settling disputes and punishing offenders. In addition, and probably more importantly, within the *kgotla*, matters affecting the

1.5 This engraving, made from a sketch taken by Robert Moffat, shows Mothibi addressing the Tlhaping *pitso* on 13 June 1823, before the battle of Dithakong.

community are discussed, and the chief, or wardhead, pronounces his decision after having heard the speeches of his people. The ruler was thus able to gauge the opinions of his most important subjects, and to act in accordance with them. If he did not, or if matters became too factionalised and he was unable to impose his will on the polity, he could expect secession. Nevertheless, if they functioned well, they could be powerful institutions. Nelson Mandela recalls that he received his initial political education, and no doubt his emphasis on the importance of conciliation, at the court of his guardian, the regent for the Thembu king.

The main task of the ruler was to preserve the prosperity of the community. In the first place, this meant ensuring that the rain fell, a matter of crucial importance, particularly west of the Drakensberg where rainfall is both less abundant absolutely, on average, and less reliable than further east. The Batswana, on the drought-ridden margins of the Kalahari, ended every speech and proclamation with the exclamation *Pula!* – let it rain – and this has become both the motto of the modern Republic of Botswana and the name of its currency. Moshoeshoe once noted that 'peace is like the rain which makes the grass grow, while war is like the wind which dries it up'. Thus a ruler could make the rain at least seem to go further by preserving peace.

There was more to it. The rain would fail or other calamities would overtake the polity, it was thought, if the land was impure or bewitched. Humans need to know why misfortunes occur, and pre-colonial South Africans could not fall back on such explanations as the periodic emergence of the *El Niño* currents off the coasts of South America, which lead to a disturbance in the world's air mass circulation, or the introduction of cattle-killing viruses from Europe, to explain drought or lung-sickness. And no one can explain why one person is struck by lightning and another not. Rather, depending on the scale of the disaster, explanations were sought at the level of the individual, the family or the polity, and evil was thought to be either the punishment of the ancestors for the faults of the living or the work of malevolent individuals, in other words witches. Ancestors could be propitiated through sacrifices, and harmony restored, but witches had to be rooted out of society. If tensions and rumours became too great, the ruler would arrange for a ceremony at which specialists smelt out the witches, who would be put to death, together with their immediate families, and their stock confiscated. Then, it was believed, harmony would be restored, and prosperity return.

These major explosions of tension were a sign that matters had gone badly wrong. In general, men and women attempted to ensure their health through forms of preventative medicine, essentially ensuring that the ancestors were well disposed to the living. When this failed, it became necessary to seek help from a specialist, who would use herbal remedies and attempt to divine whether some form of pollution had disturbed the well-being of the family. Equally, at the level of the polity, there were rituals associated with the growing of crops. As we have seen, the chief was responsible for the rain to make the crops grow, and he provided medicines for the doctoring of the fields. Also there was danger associated with the new crops, which of course became available after some months of dearth, as the previous year's resources had to be husbanded very carefully through the time of hunger. Thus the chief alone could initiate the first-fruits ceremonies, after which the harvest could begin to be consumed. These ceremonies became the major ritual expression of chiefly power. Everywhere, anyone beginning to eat the harvest before royal permission was thereby proclaiming rebellion, and would be dealt with as such. In Zululand and Swaziland, these ceremonies also involved the doctoring of the army, and in the latter case the *incwala*, as it is known, has remained one of the main ritual symbols of nationality.

These, then, were some of the main structures of South African society as it was during most of the millennium which is just ending, at least as it can be reconstructed on the basis of archaeological material and back-projection from descriptions made after the invasion of the country by European colonists. While, within the region, contacts between the various groups were manifold, links to the wider world were few. The trading world of the Indian Ocean scarcely reached further south than central Mozambique. Despite South Africa's vast gold reserves, these are not of a type that allowed exploitation at the time, and the influence of the gold-exporting states of the Zimbabwe plateau was low. Only from the early seventeenth century could over-seas trade develop, largely to the small Portuguese settlement at Delagoa Bay (modern Maputo). Through here, American crops – particularly maize – were introduced, and ivory and a very few slaves exported.

Probably as a result of the benefits that the rulers in the area could derive from this trade, the eighteenth century saw a considerable increase in the size of political units in northern KwaZulu-Natal and southern Mozambique, notably the Mabhudu kingdom just south of the Bay and the Ndwandwe and Mthethwa polities further south. In the far south, in the Ciskei and Transkei, the Xhosa and Thembu kingdoms were also expanding, although at the cost of political centralisation. Elsewhere, chiefdoms remained small. Perhaps the largest were the Tswana states along the Kalahari margin, but this may be an illusion, caused by the fact that their rulers were able to require most of their subjects to live in the central town, at least during the winter. These were thus the largest settlements in the region. In the summer, as the rains came, people dispersed out over the countryside. In general, though, South African society was fragmented as it came to confront the challenge of European colonisation from the mid-seventeenth century on.

2

Colonial conquest

After 1500, South Africa ceased to be a place at the end of the world. Once Europeans had discovered how to sail from their home countries to the southern coasts of Asia round the Cape of Good Hope, the region came to be exposed to a whole new set of influences, and eventually to European conquest and settlement.

It did not happen immediately. The killing of the Portuguese admiral, Francisco de Almeida, on the shores of Table Bay encouraged his successors to concentrate their African efforts on the east coast of the continent, well to the north of modern South Africa, whence in any event they could acquire gold, slaves and ivory not yet available to the south. When, after 1600, the Vereenigde Oost-Indisch Compagnie (the Dutch East India Company, usually known as the VOC) began to challenge the Iberians for supremacy among Europeans in Asia, its mariners discovered the advantages of sailing due east from the Cape on the reliable westerly winds before swinging north to India or Java. They could return on the south-east trade winds directly from there to Natal. As a result, their only landfall, in both directions, was in modern South Africa. The advantages for Dutch shipping of a permanent establishment on the coasts of the country soon became evident.

In 1652, then, a small party of Dutchmen under Jan van Riebeeck arrived in Table Bay. In political and constitutional terms, the modern South African state is the lineal descendant of Van Riebeeck's settlement.

Initially, the Dutch intended that their establishment should be no more than a trading post. They hoped to acquire the supplies they needed for the ships which put in to Table Bay, namely food, firewood and water, from the Khoikhoi of the neighbourhood in exchange for European commodities, or as free goods. However, within a decade or so it had become clear that even under duress the Khoikhoi were unable or unwilling to supply the meat demanded by several thousand sailors who still had a voyage of four months or so to make. Agricultural commodities, notably bread, vegetables and wine (the latter two were needed to combat scurvy) were simply not forthcoming at all. The Dutch considered they had no option but to transform their post on the shore into a genuine colony.

In order to establish such a colony, two conditions had to be met. First, the Dutch had to appropriate the land on which the Khoisan lived. This was done by force. In the early years of the settlement, two short wars were fought in which the Dutch demonstrated their technological superiority, at least when the rain did not neutralise their flintlock guns. Thereafter, their activities with regard to the main Khoikhoi chiefdoms were mainly limited to the trading and raiding of cattle and sheep. Since the authority of the Khoikhoi leaders was primarily based on their riches in stock, both of these practices had the effect of decreasing their power, and thus the cohesion of the groups they controlled and their ability to resist. With the seizure of their flocks and herds, Khoikhoi polities disintegrated as organised units.

Resistance continued, of course. Khoikhoi who had lost their cattle combined with the San of the mountains and the semi-desert of the interior to engage in a long and intermittent process of guerrilla warfare against the invading colonists. Throughout the eighteenth century, farms were raided and burnt, stock driven off and herdsmen killed. At times, the San managed to drive the Europeans from extensive tracts of land. In the 1770s, for instance, groups up to 400 strong, many of whom had previously been farm labourers, managed to clear the Europeans out of the stretch of the escarpment between modern Beaufort West and Graaff-Reinet, and out the Sneeuberge to the north of the latter town. There, the San leader Koerikei called out to the farmers:

What are you doing in my land? You have taken all the places where the eland and other game live. Why did you not stay where the sun goes down, where you first came from?

He would, he said, kill their herdsmen and chase them all away. The retribution, however, was terrible. The burgher (citizen) militias known as commandos received permission from the Cape government to 'extirpate' the San, thus formalising their genocidal practice which had been in operation for most of the century. Hundreds of San were killed in these operations, and the children were taken as *de facto* slaves.

These wars occurred during the expansion of the colony from around 1680 onwards. This could only occur after the second condition had been met, that is to say after the establishment of a social order by which the Cape could function as a colony. This required that the Cape was settled by foreigners. They were, however, of two basic legal statuses. On the one hand there were the free immigrants from Europe, most of whom had served the VOC as soldiers, sailors and artisans, often in Cape Town itself. A number of people also came to the Cape as deliberate immigrants, without any previous employment in the VOC, most notably a group of about 200 Protestant refugees from persecution in France. Some of these people made a living in Cape Town, as artisans, innkeepers, merchants and so forth. Others, including all the Huguenot French, were granted rights, effectively in ownership, to portions of the land in the colony, on which they established farms. On the other hand, there were involuntary immigrants, or slaves. In total, between the foundation of the colony in 1652 and the abolition of the overseas slave trade in 1807, about 60,000 slaves were imported into the Cape, from Indonesia, India, Madagascar and the east coast of Africa in approximately equal numbers.

Together, the masters, their slaves and those Khoisan who, under duress or otherwise, had come to work within the colonial sphere, created the tripartite structure of colonial South Africa before the nineteenth century. At the heart of the colony, though spatially at its ultimate south-west corner, was Cape Town. This was the seat of the VOC government of the colony, which was itself subservient both to the Governor-General in Batavia (Jakarta) and to the VOC's directors (the *Heren XVII*) in the Netherlands. The VOC held the ultimate power within the colony. It would occasionally discipline free burghers for excesses towards their slaves and the Khoisan, and much more frequently, and with great brutality, would maintain the authority of the free over the slaves, and of the high officials over the soldiers and sailors

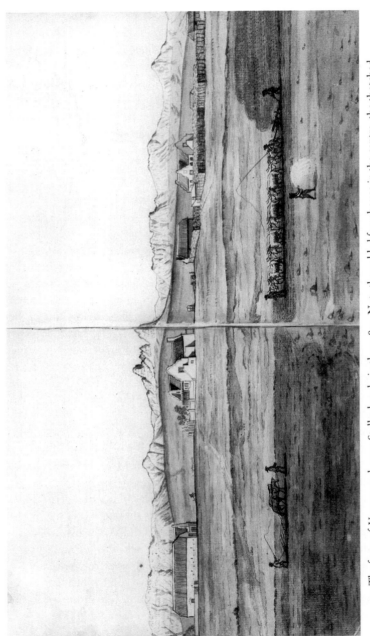

2.1 The farm of Vergenoegd, near Stellenbosch, in the 1780s. Note the gabled farmhouse in the centre, the thatched slave quarters to the right, and the ox-plough and harrow in the foreground.

in VOC service. Cape Town was also the main, virtually the only, market in the colony. Farmers brought their agricultural produce there by ox-waggon, or drove their stock to be slaughtered in the Cape Town shambles. They could purchase cloth, agricultural implements, domestic utensils, coffee, tea, sugar and slaves from Cape Town's merchants. Cape Town, with approximately a third of the colony's non-Khoisan population, was therefore its commercial, social and administrative centre.

Secondly, there were the farms of the South-West Cape. Since bulk transport of agricultural commodities was not profitable across the mountain passes of the Cape fold belt, these were limited to the valleys and plains within about 80 kilometres of Cape Town. Within this region, the classic crops of the Mediterranean complex, wine and wheat, were produced in middling size units, with ten to fifty slaves and a fair number of Khoisan as casual labourers during the harvest. Particularly towards the end of the eighteenth century, as the market became more buoyant, the farmers' prosperity allowed them to build the magnificent whitewashed and gabled farmhouses in what became known as the Cape Dutch style. These demonstrated at once the emergence of this group of farmers as a gentry with a claim to pre-eminence within rural society, and thus to participation within the political structures which were still firmly under the control of the VOC, and their dominance over their slave and Khoisan labourers. However, such symbolism could not obviate the need for the more rigorous forms of control over a labour force of slaves who accepted their bondage, if at all, as a fact of life, not as a just ordering of society.

Thirdly, from around 1690, settler farmers, above all those with little capital, began to move across the mountains to take control of the interior of the Cape. In so doing, they were primarily responsible for dispossessing the Khoisan of the land and stock, and forcing the Khoisan survivors to work for them. They themselves engaged in a certain amount of agriculture, primarily for their own consumption, but maintained their contacts with the Cape market through the sale of stock, and to some extent stock products such as butter, soap and tallow. Their great herds and flocks, of cattle and sheep of breeds which the Khoisan had created, required extensive tracts of grazing, particularly in arid lands away from the coast. They also had to move with the seasons according to patterns of transhumance which the farmers had learnt from their Khoisan herdsmen. In so doing, they lived on, and shot out, the massive herds of game of the Karoo, where they had lived on the grasses and bushy succulents of this dry region. One species of antelope, the blauwbok, and one of zebra, the quagga, were brought to extinction in the process, and several others, notably the bontebok and the mountain zebra, reduced to tiny remnant populations. They were replaced by cattle and, above all, sheep, the products of which – meat, fat, butter above all – could be marketed. However the introduction of alien species and the general decrease of bio-diversity reduced the biomass that could safely be run on the Karoo to not much more than a tenth of the original. Few if any farmers were able to withstand the temptation to exceed this, with disastrous consequences for the long-term ecology of the region.

Temporarily, though, the Cape interior was a land of plenty. The population of those of European descent doubled every generation; the area of European settlement, however thin, expanded almost as rapidly. In so doing, the farmers moved beyond the scope of effective political control by the VOC government, and its institutions were only accepted when it suited the farmers. Equally, although they, like all European settlers at the Cape, were proud of their Christianity, by force of circumstance they practised their religion within the household, and attended the churches, all in the south-west until 1786, most irregularly.

By the end of the eighteenth century, then, European descended farmers had conquered most of the territory to the west of the Fish River and to the south of the Gariep. In the east they had come into contact with the most westerly of the amaXhosa, and the war, which with many pauses lasted a century, on the eastern frontier of the Cape Colony had begun. To the north, the most advanced representatives of colonial society were not the whites, as defined within the colony, but rather people of at least partial Khoisan descent who had acquired those prime articles of colonial power, horses and guns. Many of them, later known as Griquas or Oorlams, spoke Dutch and saw Christianity as a way of legitimating their status. Along the valley of the Gariep River, and to its north, in Namibia, the Northern Cape and the Free State, they and the Korana, who did not claim European descent, established themselves and began to threaten the Sotho-Tswana or Herero chiefdoms in their neighbourhood.

From the middle of the eighteenth century, a slow political revolution occurred on the High Veld and in the valleys of the eastern coastal belt.

The causes of this are unclear, although they seem most probably to have been related to the increased demand for ivory and other products of the chase, notably leopard skins, among traders on the coast, in modern Mozambique. Again, the introduction of maize may have led to an increase in the carrying capacity of the land, but also made communities which relied on it more vulnerable to the droughts which periodically strike central South Africa. From the 1790s, the activities of raiders using horses and firearms from the Middle Gariep river, and ultimately emanating from the Cape Colony, certainly exacerbated and steered the conflicts.

However these various causes should be weighted, the consequences were clear. There was a steady rise in the size of African polities. African rulers with privileged access to the profits of trade were able to distribute the goods they had acquired, thus expanding their networks of patronage. Equally, the increase in conflict meant that those who could provide security, generally because they had settled on an easily defensible hill-top, attracted additional followers as if by capillary action.

There were two distinct phases to this process. Until the second decade of the nineteenth century, political consolidation was certainly occurring in the hinterland of Delagoa Bay, both to its south with the emergence of the Mabhudu kingdom just south of the Bay and the Ndwandwe and Mthethwa polities further south, and to its west, as Thulare, a chief whose descendants' followers would later be known as the Bapedi, came to dominate the Lydenburg plateau controlling access from the High Veld to the Bay. Similar concentrations of power are also discernible along the Kalahari edge, notably among the Bamangwato of north-east Botswana and in the south of that country, where Makaba's settling on Kanye hill around 1790 formed the basis of Ngwaketse power. This process was anything but peaceful. Both on the High Veld and to the east of the Drakensberg political consolidation involved the conquest of competitors' land and people. However, the wars in question were by no means as total as those which would follow.

After about 1820, the second phase began, marked by the degree of violence, and also by the size of the polities which emerged out of it. Two developments lay at the heart of this. First, the pressure from the south on the High Veld became more intense, as Griqua and Kora raiders grew in numbers, acquired more firearms and opened up better markets in the Cape for the products of their activities, which included a small number of *de facto* slaves. Secondly, the wars in Natal culminated in the emergence of the Zulu kingdom under Shaka. The Zulu were certainly not the prime movers in the process. Rather they were subjects of a small chiefdom which had for a time been under the suzerainty of the Mthethwa kingdom. During the 1810s, the Mthethwa had been in conflict with the amaNdwandwe, under Zwide, to their north. Shaka was able to stay out of this conflict, and thus to preserve sufficient force to resist the victorious amaNdwandwe and to defeat them in a major battle in about 1819 on the banks of the Mhlatuze river. From that moment, the Zulu kingdom under Shaka was the paramount power in what is now known as KwaZulu-Natal.

Shaka has become the most mythical figure in South African history, demonised for his bloodthirstiness and for the cruelty of the system he established, or almost deified for his military prowess, his statesmanship and his foresight. He was clearly a man endowed with the political skill, the ruthlessness and the luck needed to prosper in the highly competitive world within which he lived. Nevertheless, he was not unique. He was only one of a clutch of South African leaders who, during the first half of the nineteenth century, founded or greatly enlarged states. Moreover, the political system which he founded was an extension of the standard structures of the region. Zulu regiments, or *impi*s, were based on the solidarity of men who had been initiated together; Shaka merely strengthened their military role. The kinship-based homestead remained the economic foundation of Zulu society, and the locus for the subordination of women; successive Zulu kings intervened to influence the timing of its foundation. The political units of pre-Shakan KwaZulu survived as important foci for loyalty, and Zulu administration was based around them.

The Zulu kingdom of Shaka and his successors ruled over modern KwaZulu-Natal to the north of the Thukela river, and exerted a degree of suzerainty further south. Its effects were felt far more widely. After Zwide's defeat, the remnants of the Ndwandwe moved north, increasing the level of conflict in the region of Swaziland, Mpumalanga and southern Mozambique. At least four major leaders of KwaZulu-Natal chiefdoms fled from Shaka with sufficient followers to form the basis for their own continued rule. Madikane and his son Ncaphayi moved south into the northern Transkei, where they established the Bhaca chiefdomship. A fair number of individuals also took this route, where they were absorbed, albeit temporarily, by the amaXhosa and amaThembu.

2.2 Shaka Zulu, as drawn to the description of Nathaniel Isaacs. This heavily mythologised picture gives an idea of the image which the early European visitors, and later South Africans of all backgrounds, created of Shaka.

Mzilikazi of the amaKhumalo, Mpangazitha of the amaHlubi and Matiwane of the amaNgwane moved over the Drakensberg onto the High Veld. Mzilikazi there founded the Ndebele kingdom, named after the common Sotho-Tswana appellation of Nguni-speakers, which was first based on the Vaal river around modern Vereeniging, and then moved north into the Magaliesberg. From 1832, it was centred on the headwaters of the Limpopo in modern Northwest Province, from where it exerted a far wider influence. Matiwane, on the other hand, spent several years in the eastern Free State, before moving south to the highlands of the north-eastern Transkei. Mzilikazi was said to have accumulated two hundred thousand head of cattle during his conquests, and Matiwane undoubtedly was also rich. They were thus profitable targets for raiding, and in both cases their translocation was driven by a desire to remove themselves from the orbit of Zulu attacks. However, in the case of the Ndebele, the attentions of the Griquas and Korana proved at least as problematic, as Mzilikazi's kingdom at once attracted and provided some protection against their activities.

The movement of these groups into the Delagoa Bay hinterland, onto the High Veld and towards the Transkei increased the general level of insecurity in these regions. After the Zulu defeat of the amaNdwandwe, the level of slave exports through the Bay increased sharply, and there was a steady flow of captives and refugees from the High Veld south into the Cape Colony. In the 1820s, warfare on the High Veld, in particular, was endemic and destructive. Settlements became built for defence, in one case entirely underground in a cavern system. It is from this period that stories of cannibalism derive. Almost certainly, these are not strictly accurate, but they can be seen as metaphors for major social disorientation.

Out of this maelstrom there emerged a limited number of kingdoms, which were of a greater size than any that had preceded them. The Zulu kingdom was probably the most powerful of these. It survived the murder of Shaka by his brother Dingane in 1828 – or perhaps it survived because Shaka was murdered – and came to dominate the eastern valleys between the Thukela and the Phongolo rivers. It was however by no means the only one. To the south, in the Transkei, Faku, son of Ngqungqushe, steadily expanded the influence of the Mpondo kingdom. To the north, Sobhuza I re-established Ngwane power, first in the south of what would later be known as Swaziland, and later at

Ezulwini in the east centre of the kingdom. It would, however, only take on its modern name during the reign of his son Mswati, who ruled from 1838 to 1865. In the modern Northern Province, Sekwati could consolidate what would later be known as the Pedi kingdom in the mountain valleys of the Steelpoort river. Mzilikazi's Ndebele, as has been mentioned, came to dominate the southern Transvaal, albeit only temporarily. To the west, the various Tswana chiefdoms of the Kalahari edge reconstituted themselves, although the rise to power of the Ngwato kingdom of north-east Botswana only really occurred in the second half of the century.

In many ways, the most remarkable success was that of Moshoeshoe, the founder of the kingdom of Lesotho. He was born in about 1786, the son of the village headman of Menkhoaneng in the upper Caledon river valley, within the borders of the kingdom he later founded. Though his youth was privileged, his young adulthood was harsh. In an attempt to provide security he established himself first on Butha Buthe. Then, in 1824, he led a nightmare march in the cold of winter across 120 kilometres of mountainous country, during which Moshoeshoe's grandfather, Peete, disappeared, to Thaba Bosiu, the 'Mountain of Night'. This flat-topped hill rises about a hundred metres above the valley floor and is a little over a square kilometre in size. It is entirely surrounded by overhanging sandstone cliffs, except for a few narrow passes, where basalt dikes allow a difficult ascent. Since food could be stored on the summit, and there is a good spring of water, it was effectively impregnable, at least until the arrival of Europeans able to bombard it with mortar shells. Like many capitals of Southern African kingdoms, it is also near an ecological boundary, between the fertile lowlands of the Caledon river valley and the Maluti mountains, into which stock could be sent for security in times of war.

Moshoeshoe was clearly a man of forceful personality, easily accepted as a leader. He had, after all, taken over the leadership of a small band of followers while his father was still alive. He also displayed a degree of statecraft, within the parameters of Southern African tradition, which was almost unparalleled. He did not eschew force; shortly after settling on Thaba Bosiu, he sent two expeditions south over the Drakensberg to lift cattle from the Thembu. The herds he acquired were then loaned out to followers under the *mafisa* system, whereby the recipients received the milk from the cattle and a proportion of the

2.3 Thaba Bosiu, as seen from afar in 1834.

2.4 Moshoeshoe, 1845, portrait by François Maeder.

natural increase as a basis for their own herds, while Moshoeshoe enjoyed their loyalty and the benefits of dispersing his own cattle. In this and other ways, he encouraged the scattered peoples of the High Veld to come under his protection. His new subjects might be of all origins, Nguni as well as Sotho-Tswana, and Moshoeshoe spoke both languages. He tied his new subjects further to him by a wide network of marriages. His hospitality was legendary, exemplified in the myth, which may have been true, that he accepted the cannibals who had captured and eaten his grandfather, rejecting calls that he put them to death with the statement that one does not desecrate the graves of one's ancestors, and giving them land. Slowly, though, his brothers and his sons were installed as chiefs throughout his domains, thus extending the authority of the royal house.

From the 1830s, the Basotho of Moshoeshoe began to take over European goods, notably blankets, which allowed settlement in the frosts of the mountains, horses and guns. These were acquired with the proceeds from the sale of grain. Moshoeshoe himself also built up a close relationship with the missionaries of the Paris Evangelical Missionary Society, notably Eugène Casalis who came to live at the foot of Thaba Bosiu. He himself continually put off his own baptism, finally dying in 1870 two days before the ceremony was to take place. Nevertheless, the missionaries saw him as a model chief, and willingly acted as his diplomatic intermediaries in his dealings with the British colonial rulers. As will be shown later in this chapter, this was an increasingly vital relationship for all South African leaders.

This illustrates a point of more general relevance. The successful African rulers of the mid-nineteenth century were those who, on the one hand, were able to exploit the possibilities within South African political systems for increasing the size of their adherence, but, on the other, also had access to resources, material or otherwise, which derived from the presence of Europeans beyond their borders. Thus, successive Zulu rulers profited from the presence of European traders, and later a European colony, to their south. After the 1830s, the amaSwati were able to benefit by selling slaves to the republics of the interior, and to Delagoa Bay. The Bapedi exported labour to the south. The various Tswana kings exploited their favourable connections with missionaries, both to manipulate their external relations and to give them extra resources of command over their subjects. In consequence, the later conquest of the South African interior was made more difficult by the previous contacts which African rulers had had with the advance guard of colonial penetration.

There is one further point which needs to be made. I have argued that political allegiance lay at the basis of ethnic identity. If this is the case, then it is important to realise that the polities to which South Africans owed allegiance were almost all of nineteenth-century creation, or at the very least expanded greatly in that time. Thus, however they were later elaborated, South African ethnicities are in general of relatively recent origin.

In 1795, the British conquered the Cape as part of their general campaign to secure their hegemony over the world's seas in the course of their war with revolutionary France. In 1803 the colony was returned to the Batavian Republic, as the Dutch state was then called. Three years later, after war had broken out again and with the Netherlands still under French influence, the British once again captured the colony. This time, they would maintain their control well after the Battle of Waterloo.

The incorporation of the Cape Colony into the British Empire greatly affected the whole tenor of social and political relations within the Colony. To begin with the latter, the British maintained the existing system of law, so that the basis of the South African legal system to this day is the Roman-Dutch law of the pre-revolutionary Netherlands. The codification which occurred in Europe under Napoleon was not incorporated. The British also based their political rule on a continued alliance with the major landowners of the colony, eschewing, at least in the short term, any major transformation of rural (or for that matter urban) social relations. Against this, incorporation in the British empire allowed for the expansion of the colony's commercial relations, as the restrictions which had still been in place under the last years of VOC rule were lifted. In particular, the early nineteenth century saw a substantial increase in wine production, for export to what was a somewhat protected British market. At the same time, wool-bearing merino sheep, the first of which had actually arrived in the colony before 1795 and which were well adapted to the arid grazing of much of the Cape, were introduced into many areas, first in the southern plains and later in the Eastern Cape. Together with the steady expansion of coastal shipping, this progressively conquered the tyrannical inadequacies of transport to allow the greater commercialisation of the Cape. The process was speeded up by the importation of British capital and British immigrants, who arrived at first as individuals but in 1820 as a large group of assisted settlers.

In the first third of the nineteenth century, British imperial actions were justified, to the British themselves, by claims that they would, or at least should, make the world a better place. This entailed intervention to quell what were for the first time seen as abuses. Thus, from 1808 the slave trade to British colonies was forbidden. This certainly affected the demographic development of the slave population and may well have given added incentives to the full incorporation of the Khoisan as labourers within Cape society, to the extent that this had not already been completed. As part of the same ameliorative impulse, the British also regulated the relationship between the Khoisan labourers and their employers. However, even if they may have diminished the incidence of naked violence between farmer and Khoi, the codes issued by Governors the Earl of Caledon in 1809 and Sir John Cradock in 1812 left the balance so heavily in favour of the employers that they eventually formed a major butt of humanitarian agitation.

The main publicists of this agitation were missionaries, in an attempt to make colonial society one in which it would be possible for their converts to live what they conceived of as proper Christian lives. The first missionary had arrived in the Colony in 1736. Georg Schmidt, the man in question, was a member of the Moravian Brotherhood. Although he was sponsored by influential figures in the Dutch East India Company in Amsterdam, he soon fell foul of the Cape clergy and authorities, and was forced to return to Europe after only seven years. In 1792, missions were restarted, again by Moravians, who established South Africa's first mission station where Schmidt had worked at Baviaans Kloof – later renamed Genadendal, the valley of Grace – some hundred miles east of Cape Town. The Moravians were quickly followed by other missionaries sponsored by British non-conformists, both Methodists and the putatively interdenominational – but actually Congregationalist – London Missionary Society. By the 1830s they had been joined by a wide range of other Protestants, of British, German and French Huguenot extraction.

Three factors aided this expansion, which by that period had made the Cape probably the most heavily missionised area in the world. First, the climate was healthy for Europeans, so that the missionaries did not die as quickly as they did, for instance, in West Africa. Secondly, the colony provided a social infrastructure under which the network of missions could flourish easily. Thirdly, and probably most importantly, the early missions were remarkably successful. The network of mission stations provided the Khoisan with refuges from the harsh exploitation of the farms. The message of the missionaries also provided people whose

2.5 The Rev. Prosper Lemue addressing his congregation at
Motito, North-West Province, in 1834.

world had been shattered by the experience of colonisation with new
certainties and new ways in which to give meaning to their lives and to
interpret the world.

The power of evangelical humanitarians in Britain, whose allies a
number of the South African missionaries were, resulted in a major
restructuring of the legal relationships in the Colony. First, in 1828, all
legal disabilities on the free people of colour, particularly the Khoisan,
were removed by Ordinance 50. The impulse for this measure, which was
passed in Cape Town but later entrenched by the government in London,
derived from the superintendent of the London Missionary Society, Dr
John Philip. He argued that, by preventing the Khoisan from taking their
labour freely to the market, existing arrangements sinned against newly
developed economic precepts and were therefore unjust and, by reducing the sum of wealth and thus increasing poverty, profoundly immoral.
Similar impulses lay behind the second major restructuring, namely the
abolition of slavery. In the campaign for abolition South Africa played a
minor role, but the colony benefited from the repulsion in Britain of
Caribbean slavery. As a result, on 1 December 1834 all slaves in the Cape
were liberated, although the ex-slaves still had to endure four years of
bondage as so-called apprentices before they could enjoy their freedom.
Some managed to move to the mission stations, and others left the farms

for the small towns. There were a few places where ex-slaves managed to become independent share-croppers, or very small peasants. Attempts were made to ensure that the women and children stayed out of the formal labour process, not always successfully. In general, though, a high proportion of the ex-slaves remained working as farm labourers. Their consolation was that they were now being paid for their labour and that they could, to a degree, choose for whom they worked. After 1841, however, their conditions of labour were determined by the Master and Servants Ordinance, labour legislation heavily weighted in favour of the employers which was to be exported to the other colonies in the region and maintained long after Union.

The coming of the British also profoundly altered the balance of the relationship between the colony and the Africans beyond its borders. In the earliest clashes between the amaXhosa and the European settlers, neither party was clearly the master. Xhosa numerical advantages cancelled out European technical superiority, and neither had the logistical capability to mount long campaigns. Nor was the distinction between the two groups absolute. Europeans were on occasion used by one Xhosa party in the course of its struggle with another. The frontier between the colony and the Africans was still imprecisely defined, both spatially and socially. Once, from 1811 onwards, the British army was used in the conflicts on the eastern frontier, this parity was shattered. The organisation required to maintain an army in the field, to feed it and to move it around was something which the amaXhosa could not manage. The British were thus able to win their wars by reducing the amaXhosa to poverty, burning their fields and huts and driving off their cattle. At times, and for a time, matters might not be so clear-cut. In 1819, for instance, Xhosa forces almost managed to capture Grahamstown, and early in the war of 1834–5 a wide swathe of farmhouses was laid to waste. Such successes were always of short duration, though, as eventually sufficient European troops could be called up to crush further Xhosa resistance. This was done with callous brutality, epitomised not just by the burning of homesteads but also by the murder and decapitation of the Xhosa king, Hintsa, in 1835, after he had begun negotiations to end a war in which he himself had played virtually no part.

Despite the destruction that they caused, the wars on the Eastern Frontier of the colony were not altogether unwelcome to many of the settlers. In the short term, they provided considerable economic opportunities. Contracts for supplying the British army lay at the basis of numerous individual fortunes. Indeed only because of the money spent by the British army (and by the naval base at Simonstown, near Cape Town) could the colony pay for what it imported. In the somewhat longer term, the wars meant that more land was available to the settlers, and particularly to the burgeoning wool industry in the Eastern Cape. The removal of a large tract of such land, when the Kat River valley, from which the Xhosa chief Maqoma was driven in 1829, was used to settle Khoi families, led to much enmity between the inhabitants of the Kat River Settlement, as it was known, and the sheep-farming gentry based on Grahamstown. An even greater shock occurred in 1836, when the Colonial Office in London ordered the restitution to the amaXhosa of Queen Adelaide Province, the mass of the modern Ciskei, which had been taken under colonial rule in the war a year earlier.

The destruction caused during the war of 1834–5 and its outcome, little favourable to the colonists, were among the causes of the Great Trek, the movement out of the colony of several thousand of its Dutch-speaking inhabitants, now known as Afrikaner. They were of course not the only ones. There had been increasing displeasure at the policy of the British in South Africa, notably at Ordinance 50 and the emancipation of slaves which were seen as proof of the influence over the colony of British missionaries, notably Dr Philip of the LMS. At the same time, the pressure of population among the Afrikaners of the Eastern Cape and the demand for land to be used for sheep farming was leading to an inexorable spread of white settlement to the north. Young men attempting to set themselves up as independent farmers were finding it increasingly difficult to appropriate land on which to begin their operations. Already by the 1820s they were beginning to settle north of the Gariep River, to the impotent displeasure of the colonial government which had intended to maintain the river as the colony's northern border.

The Great Trek was thus the consequence of a combination of the long-term northward movement of the farmers with the specific events of the late 1820s and 1830s. Its result was a massive increase in the extent of that proportion of modern South Africa dominated by people of European descent. It was thus one of the crucial events in the formation of the country.

In the course of 1836, bands of Voortrekkers, as they have come to be known, were beginning to coalesce in the grasslands around the Vaal River. Certain individuals, notably Hendrik Potgieter, Piet Retief, Gert Maritz and Sarel Cilliers, emerged as the trekkers' leaders, largely on the basis of their wealth and the prestige that they had had in the Cape Colony. As they moved north, the trekkers ignored a warning that they should obtain permission from Mzilikazi before they crossed the Vaal. The Ndebele ruler certainly saw the trekkers in much the same terms as the Griqua under Barend Barends who had been raiding them from the south for several years. Mzilikazi sent several *impi*s against them, destroying a number of camps and capturing large numbers of the cattle which the Voortrekkers had brought with them. During the course of these encounters, however, the Voortrekkers learnt to perfect the defensive military technique of corralling their waggons into a *laager* which was to prove impenetrable for the spear-wielding African infantrymen, at least as long as the Voortrekkers were able to keep up a rapid fire from the muzzle loaded guns. Equally, horsemen with guns could usually escape from any number of their unmounted adversaries.

After the initial clashes, the Voortrekkers allied with the Griqua and Korana and with those Tswana who had been displaced and harassed by the Ndebele over the previous years. A series of attacks was launched, particularly against the fertile Mosega basin in the headwaters of the Limpopo. These were then followed by a major raid launched over the Drakensberg by the Zulu. In consequence, Mzilikazi and the Ndebele decided that they could no longer maintain their position in the southern Transvaal, and moved *en masse* to the north, finally settling in what was to become south-west Zimbabwe. The Voortrekkers had created a power vacuum to the north of the Vaal.

At this point there was a division among the Voortrekkers. One portion consisted of those who decided to remain on the High Veld. Towards the south, there was a steady increase in commercial sheep farming, so that the area to the north of the Gariep was economically merely an extension of that to the south. At the same time, the Griquas who had settled around Philippolis were following the same path. Although on occasions there were attempts on the part of the Voortrekkers to forge an alliance with the Philippolis Griquas, in general, and in continuation of the Cape practice there was distrust and competition between the two groups. Further north, sheep did not do so well, and the old South African problems of transporting bulk goods made agriculture an unattractive proposition for the immigrants – even if there had been a major market for maize or sorghum. The exploitation of an African peasantry and of captured *inboekelinge* (effectively slaves) ensured the trekkers' subsistence, but for the generation of a cash income they were long dependent on the products of hunting. A number of small communities were established. The most settled was that in the south-west Transvaal, centred on Potchefstroom, while those in the north and east, around the Zoutpansberg and Lydenburg, were always small and vulnerable. It was their privileged access to guns and powder, and their close and mutually advantageous relations with the Swazi monarchy, which ensured their survival.

The other main group of trekkers, probably a majority initially, moved south-east across the Drakensberg into what is now KwaZulu-Natal. This meant that they came into conflict with the Zulu kingdom, now under Dingane, Shaka's assassin and successor. Once it became plain that the trekkers were intending to settle in Natal, Dingane attempted to rid himself of them, having some seventy men, including the leader Piet Retief, executed for their arrogance in February 1838 during a visit to his capital uMgungundlovu and despatching his *impi*s to wipe out the rest. This failed, as the *laager* of the trekkers was able to resist the attacks, until, after a very hard winter, they managed to defeat a major force at the battle of Ncome River (later known to the whites as Blood River). Thereafter, the trekkers became the dominant force in Natal to the south of the Thukela river and two years later they sponsored and aided Mpande, Dingane's younger brother, in overthrowing the Zulu king and establishing his own rule.

The establishment of trekker power in Natal south of the Thukela threatened the small British trading community at Port Natal (Durban). More importantly, while he was no doubt aware of the vague possibility that Natal could be used to threaten British strategic control of the sea routes to the east, the British Colonial Secretary of the day, Lord Stanley, was fearful of the chaos and exploitation which trekker control would entail and therefore in 1842 authorised the annexation of the region as a British colony – less chaotic, perhaps, but in hindsight no less exploitative. Some of the trekkers remained in Natal, on the farms they were claiming, but the majority viewed English rule as an evil from which they had escaped. Led by Andries Pretorius, who had been the

2.6 Andries Pretorius consoling Piet Retief's widow, Maria
Johanna de Wet, after the battle of Ncome river, as depicted in a
silent film made in 1916 under the inspiration of Gustav Preller.
Preller was largely responsible for the creation of the visual
image of the Voortrekkers, which was to become one of the
central icons of Afrikaner nationalism. It is presented in bas-
relief on the Voortrekker monument, outside Pretoria, and would
be seen to the greatest extent in the re-enactments of the Trek in
1938 and again, with tragedy repeating itself as farce, in 1988.

The creation of the Afrikaner past as legend also entailed the
creation of Afrikaner women as mothers of the nation, as its
greatest patriots and as those who maintained its purity. This
entailed the continued relegation of Afrikaner womenfolk to the
private sphere, to work in the home and the church. There were
occasional Afrikaner feminists, but they could not compete with
the male dominance of Afrikaner – indeed of most of South
African – society.

commandant at Blood River, they returned back across the mountains
to strengthen trekker presence on the High Veld.

The logic which had led the British to annex Natal also applied west
of the Drakensberg. Hesitantly at first, the British government began to
assert its presence north of the Gariep, establishing a resident in the new
town of Bloemfontein in 1846. Two years later, after a lightning tour of
the area, the new governor Sir Harry Smith decided to declare all those

regions which the trekkers had occupied as British territory. There was considerable opposition to this on the part of the trekkers, and Sir Harry had to fight the battle of Boomplaas before British authority in what he named the Orange River Sovereignty was accepted. From then on, however, at least the southern portion of Transorangia, the modern Free State, was firmly within the British colonial ambit, and the Eastern Cape wool farmers and capitalists, mainly of British 1820 settler origin, began to take possession of its farms.

By 1850, the main contours of colonial society had been set. Throughout the Cape and in the fledgling colony of Natal it was held together by an intensifying network of trading links, still largely on the basis of ox-waggons. The opening of coasting traffic along the southern coast, and to a lesser extent north of Cape Town, meant that the problems inherent in such a system were greatly decreased, and a major programme of road building in the 1840s made many of the mountain passes less horrific. Wool had replaced wheat and wine as the colony's main export, though the growth of the internal market had meant that wheat remained the largest earner for the agricultural community as a whole. The wool was produced above all in the Eastern Province, and was shipped out through the growing harbour of Port Elizabeth. The financing and banking services which made this possible were nevertheless still centred on Cape Town, though they were operated through a wide network of local banks. These were to be found in the numerous small towns springing up throughout the colonies, which provided a range of commercial and artisanal services unheard of at the beginning of the century, including local newspapers, and which formed the social, administrative and increasingly political centres of local society.

These small towns, or *dorps* as they were known, were generally established around a Dutch Reformed Church. Before 1786, the DRC was, it is true, the only Christian denomination allowed in the colony, but it had few clergymen and, until 1786, none outside the far south-west of the country. The white inhabitants thought of themselves as Christians, and were careful to acquire membership of the church and to have their children baptised. If they could read – and probably a majority were literate – they studied the Bible carefully. After 1810, though, the density of churches became far greater, as the colony became more prosperous and also because the British hoped to anglicise the farmers, to a certain extent, by bringing in Scottish clergymen.

2.7 Colesberg, a typical Cape *dorp*, as drawn by Charles Bell in 1834. This sketch was taken during *Nagmaal*, the quarterly celebration of Holy Communion in the *Nederduits Gereformeerde Kerk*, when the farmers from the surrounding area would come into the *dorp*, for the religious service, to renew social contacts, to sell and to make the purchases necessary for the maintenance of their households and farms.

The six parishes that there had been in 1795 had grown to twenty-five by 1840, to thirty-six by 1850 and to sixty-four by 1860, excluding those which were established north of the Orange and in Natal. The church thus acquired a centrality in the life of rural communities which it had never enjoyed until then.

While it retained the adherence of the great majority of the Dutch, the DRC lost its monopoly over the religious life of the colony. British non-conformists, initially above all Wesleyan Methodists, were the pioneers, but were quickly followed by the Anglicans and, somewhat later, by the Roman Catholics. By mid-century, the country towns had four or five churches, and sometimes more. These would usually include at least one mission chapel, serving not just those who had come to the towns from the mission stations but also those ex-slaves who had moved away from the farms, and also an increasing number of farm labourers in the surrounding countryside. Outside of Cape Town, the country was becoming almost exclusively Christian. Within the city, though, and in a few other places, Islam gained numerous adherents, particularly among slaves and former slaves, after men of Asian origin had been allowed to found the first mosque in 1800.

Concomitant with this religious expansion and diversification was a slow process of cultural change among the colonial population. Schooling became much more widely available, and indeed the main work of the missionaries in many of the small towns was in fact running a school. After emancipation, the ex-slaves in particular made great efforts to learn to read and write, seeing this as a way of effectuating their freedom. For the more prosperous, a number of secondary schools were set up, which might attract people from a wide area. At least one girl from the Free State learnt 'accomplishments', though little more, in an Academy for Young Ladies in Grahamstown. More high-powered secondary education was increasingly available for boys, notably with the foundation of the South African College in Cape Town in 1829, which later developed into the University of Cape Town (and the South African College School), and also of a number of Anglican schools, notably the Diocesan College ('Bishop's'), around 1850.

Education and Christianity were among the main components of respectability, the criteria by which those who were acceptable in society were distinguished from the disreputable. In outward terms, respectability was signalled by clothing in European style, a certain standard

2.8 During the course of the nineteenth century, Islam in Cape Town became more institutionalised. Mosques were built and a written literature of religious works was produced, including the *Bayan Ud-din* (Explanation of the Religion) by Abu Bakr Effendi, a section of which is reproduced here. In general these were not in Arabic, but rather phonetic renderings, as far as was possible, of the Dutch spoken at the Cape into Arabic letters. They thus provide an insight into the form of the language at the time, uncontaminated by High Dutch orthography and grammar. This was one of the versions of Dutch ancestral to modern Afrikaans. These all developed out of the contact between Dutch-speaking colonists and individuals, of both slave and Khoi status or descent, for whom this was a second language, or they were the *linguae francae* of these speech communities. The forerunners of Afrikaans were thus initially stigmatised as the tongues of the unlettered lower orders, who did not know the rules of Dutch. From the 1870s, however, colonial nationalists came to see Afrikaans as the true bearer of their (white) culture, and in 1920 it replaced Dutch as one of the official languages of the country. For this, the language was tidied up and standardised. In the process it became much more like Dutch than the heavily creolised dialects that had preceded it.

of housing, public sobriety and so forth. Central to it, however, was a redefinition of the respective roles of men and women. Distinction there had of course always been. Dutch families in South Africa had been characterised by the pre-eminence of male household heads, but both the legal arrangements for property, which was held in common by the partners in a marriage, and the general practice of running farms and businesses gave women a measure of standing outside the specifically domestic sphere. In the course of the nineteenth century, in contrast, the division between the public and the private became stronger; in part because with the emergence of politics the public sphere became much more pronounced, and at least outside the operation of farms women were increasingly confined to the private sphere. This was not always experienced as a restriction. Particularly those women who had been slaves, or Khoisan *de facto* bondswomen, grasped the ideology of respectability to allow their escape from the sexual exploitation and the regime of unfree labour they had experienced hithertofore.

One of the groups which embraced the ideology of respectability eagerly was the mission Khoi of the Eastern Cape. For them, respectability was what was entailed by the requirement to live a Christian life. In addition, the missionaries had argued that if they demonstrated what was considered their civilisation they would receive political benefits. In the first instance, it seemed as though the missionaries could deliver on their promises, as demonstrated by the passing of Ordinance 50. By the late 1840s, this enthusiasm had dampened. The frontier wars of 1835–6 (Hintsa's war) and 1846–7 (the War of the Axe) had destroyed much of their property. Antagonism against them from European settlers was growing. Their economic advance was blocked by white discrimination and rumours were flying around that the introduction of a parliament into the Cape, dominated as it would be by settlers, would lead to their return to a state of near-slavery. It is thus not surprising that a proportion of the Eastern Cape Khoi, from the Kat River, from the mission villages of Theopolis and Shiloh and also from the farms, joined with the Xhosa against the colonists in the war which broke out in 1850.

This event, known somewhat erroneously as the Kat River Rebellion, thus intersected with the two most salient processes in South African history in the decade after 1848. The first was constitutional reform. From about 1830, some of the colonists in the Cape had been agitating for more influence over the government. Successive Colonial Secretaries in London had refused this because of the danger of entrusting South African affairs to a parliament of men who had been slave-owners or were in other ways known to be hostile to the black population of the colony and the lands beyond its borders. In this they were supported by the liberals in the colony. By the late 1840s, both sources of opposition had disappeared. In 1846 the Whigs returned to power in Britain. As the party which had benefited most from the property-holding democracy instituted by the Great Reform Act of 1832, they naively believed that similar provisions could only bring about justice in South Africa. Equally, the liberals in the colony were repelled by the authoritarian nature of Cape government, particularly after the attempt to introduce a shipload of convicts into the colony. Furthermore, ethnic tensions between English and Dutch had been defused by the tacit decision of the Dutch elite to avoid stressing their nationality, on the reasonable assumption that they would dominate any parliament introduced into the colony.

In 1848, then, the British announced that a legislative assembly would be instituted in the Cape Colony. It would be based on a property franchise, and the main question to be determined was the level of that franchise. In the event it was decided, after considerable wrangling, that all adult male householders occupying fixed property worth a minimum of £25 would be eligible for the vote. When this was finally put through, in 1853, it gave the Cape one of the most 'democratic' constitutions in the world at the time, one whereby most Dutch men, and a fair number of 'coloureds' as the ex-slaves and Khoisan were beginning to be called, could vote. At no stage in the sixty-six-year history of the Cape Parliament, however, was a coloured man elected, in part because a man with the prestige to be elected was no longer considered coloured. (Both the country's first baronet, Andries Stockenström, and its first member of the British House of Lords, J.H. de Villiers, fell into this category.) It was only in a handful of constituencies that they, or later the Africans, were able to influence substantially the choice of their representative.

In parallel with this process, Great Britain reorganised its relationships with those Europeans who had left the colony to the north. In Natal, the aided settlement of English men and women began to replace those of Dutch descent who had moved back over the mountains. On the High Veld, the British realised that their rash assumption of sovereignty over the lands between the Gariep and Vaal had been a mistake. On the one hand, it brought the British no nearer to controlling the trekkers to the north of the Vaal river. On the other, it embroiled them in the very complicated politics of the Caledon river valley, forcing them to ally with the European settlers and certain African groups, notably the Barolong of Thaba Nchu, against Moshoeshoe and the Basotho, over whom they had nominal, but totally ineffectual, control. In the subsequent wars, the British-led forces suffered one significant defeat, at Viervoet (Kononyana, to give it its Sotho name) in 1851, and a year later, after British troops had been moved north, escaped from the battle of the Berea with dignity only because Moshoeshoe saw no profit in pushing matters to the ultimate conclusion. In consequence, the British retreated from north of the Gariep, first by the Sand River Convention of 1852 recognising disparate groups of farmers as the South African Republic, generally known as the Transvaal, and then in 1854 establishing the Orange Free State by the Bloemfontein Convention.

In both cases, the arrangements of the new states were rigged to ensure the formal dominance of people of European descent, although Lesotho was removed from a European control which had only been nominal. In the Transvaal, it was only in the south and parts of the east that any such control was achieved, and even there the institutions of government were for some decades very weak, and *burgher* society riven by conflict. The Boers, as the trekkers came to be known after they began to settle, could claim land, and the notables did so in large quantities, while a number of land companies were granted concessions. In general, though, these only held land in the expectation that its price would rise, and in the meantime got such income as they could from exploiting African peasants. In the Free State, in contrast, the great concentrations of land built up by those with government contacts during the Orange River Sovereignty began to be dispersed, and sheep-farming, at least in the south and centre, developed. With this went an administration which, if on a small scale, was reasonably efficient. The anomaly of the Griquas around Philippolis, who were land-owning, sheep-farming settlers within the State's borders who were nonetheless not citizens, disappeared in 1861, as the Griquas considered the pressure on them to be too great and trekked over the mountains to the north-east of the Transkei. The conflict with the Basotho on its eastern border remained endemic, as both sides contested the rich lands of the Caledon river valley. In the first clash, in 1858, the Basotho fought the Free State to a draw, at least, tying up the main force before Thaba Bosiu and launching sweeping raids against Boer farms in its rear. Ten years later, in contrast, the same basic strategy failed as the Free State brought up sufficient artillery to pound the mountain fortress, in which cattle had been gathered and now perished from hunger, and had sufficient resolve to devastate Sotho crops. After protracted negotiations, shortly before his death in 1870, Moshoeshoe agreed to the incorporation of his kingdom into the Cape Colony, but his son Letsie could only rule over a truncated realm, which had lost all land on the right bank of the Caledon.

The second major process of the late 1840s and 1850s took place among the amaXhosa. The retrocession of Queen Adelaide Province in 1836 and the treaties made between the colony and Xhosa chiefs thereafter solved little. Settler demand for Xhosa land and African labour continued to grow. A series of droughts in the 1840s exacerbated the tensions, as droughts always do in South Africa. Eventually, and inevitably, the War of the Axe, named after the incident which triggered it, broke out in 1846. This time, on no better grounds than a decade earlier, both the humanitarians in South Africa and the British Government were convinced that the war was the result of Xhosa actions. They had, then, no scruples about retaining Xhosaland east of the Kei river, and thus, for the first time in the history of the country – indeed, of the continent – substantial populations of Africans with their social structures more or less intact were brought under colonial rule.

In the War of the Axe, the British made use of African auxiliaries from the group known as amaMfengu. These people had left Xhosaland during and after the 1835 war to throw in their lot with the colony. They consisted both of those who had come from Natal in flight from Shaka's wars and had remained, unassimilated, among the amaXhosa for a few years and, probably in smaller numbers, of individuals and families who had rejected the structures of Xhosa society, or at least their own place within it. They were already the missions' leading converts, and would also be among the first to take up commercial agriculture.

For the mass of the amaXhosa, both east and west of the Kei, the defeat in the War of the Axe and the beginnings of colonial rule undermined their certainties. As was argued in the previous chapter, chiefly rule had been predicated on the ownership and distribution of cattle, now in short supply after over 40,000 head had been seized as reparations. It also entailed the rooting out of the witches who caused misfortune. This, more than anything else, was forbidden by colonial rulers, notably the governor, Sir Harry Smith, who expounded their own values as universal truths and humiliated Xhosa rulers. This might have been ignored were it not that evil was so evidently abroad. The disasters of the war and of the droughts, which returned in 1850, showed this. New ways had to be found to combat malevolence.

In these circumstances, the prophet Mlanjeni announced that he had the medicines to drive out witchcraft. He set up gateways of poles, through which witches could not pass, and he was then able to purge those who failed the test of their evil. Thus revitalised and purified, the Xhosa nation could drive out the Europeans, particularly as Mlanjeni was able to turn their bullets into hot water, at least when aimed against the pure. In alliance with the Khoi rebels from the Kat river and the colony, the amaXhosa began to clear their land. Mlanjeni's promises did not materialise, but nevertheless the amaXhosa were able to fight the longest and most costly war of resistance in their history. Better armed than ever before, and with the aid of Khoi deserters from the British army, who were obviously well trained in the use of firearms – though of course they were still seriously outgunned by the British – the Xhosa use of natural cover, particularly in the Waterkloof to the west of the Kat River and in the Amatole mountains, enabled them regularly to ambush British forces and to launch raids deep into the colony. In this they were led by Maqoma, one of the senior chiefs, who had schooled himself into the sharpest tactician and strategist the amaXhosa – or probably any South African people – produced, and who revenged himself for the particular insults he had received from Sir Harry Smith.

It could not last. The British army finally smashed its way through Xhosaland, executing its captives summarily, burning crops and seizing cattle. Then, after the amaXhosa had surrendered, they seized much of their land and, on what remained, installed magistrates in an attempt to control the chiefs and to bring what they saw as civilisation to the amaXhosa. To add to the disasters, in 1855 lungsickness hit the amaXhosa's cattle, killing two-thirds of the stock in some areas and virtually wiping out the herds of even cattle-rich chiefs. Clearly, the land was heavily polluted and drastic measures were required to restore it to health.

2.9 Maqoma, painted by Frederick I'ons, to demonstrate that he
was a worthy opponent for the British.

The solution was provided by two strangers, Sifuba-Sibanzi (the
Broad-Chested One) and Napakade (the Eternal One). These two gods,
who were Xhosa interpretations of the stories they had heard of Jesus
Christ, appeared to a young girl, Nongqawuse, near the Gxarha river in
the Transkei. They told her that if the Xhosa slaughtered all their cattle
and destroyed all their grain and all their pots then the world would
become again as new. The ancestors would return bringing with them

herds of wonderful beasts, the newly dug grain pits would fill up, the whites would disappear into the sea and all would be well. After some hesitation and only after the king, Sarhili, had declared his adherence to the prophecies, perhaps 90 per cent of the amaXhosa slaughtered their cattle, destroyed their grain, or consumed it as beer, and on the morning of 17 February 1857, waited for the ancestors and the cattle to return. Given South African ideas of pollution, and the great crisis the amaXhosa were in, this is at least intelligible.

They were disappointed. Nongqawuse is now seen as having inaugurated, not the renewal, but the mass suicide of the amaXhosa. Forty thousand died of starvation. As many again had to leave Xhosaland to seek work in the Cape Colony. The colonial government gleefully seized the opportunity of the so-called Cattle-Killing – destruction of grain was as important, economically if not symbolically – in order to force the amaXhosa into wage labour. Sir George Grey, the governor, purported to believe that the chiefs had set up the killing as a plot to induce their followers to attack the colony. He arrested most of the leading chiefs and shipped them off to prison on Robben Island. So efficiently did he exploit the Cattle-Killing that many Xhosa today are convinced that Grey himself was hiding in the reeds by the Gxarha, whispering to Nongqawuse.

As a simple statement of historical fact they are mistaken, but not if it is taken as a metaphor – and oral texts of history deal above all in metaphors. The Cattle-Killing marks the end of the beginning of South African history. For the first time, an African society (other than the Khoikhoi) had been broken. Much land had already gone, but now Africans began moving out as labourers, while paying heed to the message of the missionaries as never before. It was a process which was to be repeated, less dramatically, throughout the rest of the country.

3

Unification

It is a fascinating, but ultimately futile, exercise to speculate on what sort of country South Africa would have become if the processes at work before 1860 had continued under the same conditions. But it was not to be. In 1867, on the banks of the Vaal river just above its confluence with the Gariep, the Boers and Griquas began to find diamonds. From then on, mining, and the industry associated with it, would always be at the centre of South African economic, social and political life.

The initial alluvial diggings on the river banks would not have had the capacity to bring about such a change. Within a few years, however, in four locations close to each other between the Vaal and the Gariep, volcanic pipes were discovered in which, in the distant past, the diamonds had crystallised. These pipes, of up to twelve hectares on the surface tapering down to less than two and a half deep in the ground, were of effectively unlimited capacity. Between them, the town of Kimberley developed rapidly, to become within a very few years the second largest settlement in Southern Africa, producing 80 per cent of the region's exports.

The mines were in an area which had been claimed by both the Griquas of Griquatown and the Orange Free State. It was soon annexed, together with the rest of Griqualand – strictly speaking Griqualand West – by the Cape Colony, who were able to claim that the border with the Free State ran, not altogether coincidentally, about a mile to the east of the mines. The mining ground in each pipe was parcelled out into a large number of claims, 470 initially in the Kimberley mine, each of about 90 square metres, and even these were sold off in portions until the smallest were less than 30 square metres in area. This may not have caused too many problems as the miners excavated the surface, but matters became much difficult as they went deeper into the diamondiferous blue ground. The removal of the matrix in which the diamonds were found was only possible when aerial ropeways were installed. Walkways between the claims collapsed. The mines flooded. If the men – they were all men – who owned the claims were to become rich, they needed to solve a variety of problems.

The first, of course, was the need for labour. By the mid-1870s 50,000 African men a year sought work in Kimberley. They came from every community within Southern Africa, except for the Venda and Zulu kingdoms, but by far the largest number were Bapedi and other Sotho-Tswana speakers from the Transvaal, who had indeed been going south on migrant labour well before the discovery of diamonds, followed by Vatsonga, mainly living in what is now Mozambique, and Basotho from the mountain kingdom. There were relatively few from the Cape or Natal, and those who did come were mainly educated and Christian, employed as artisans and clerks. Those who sought unskilled employment could find it closer to home, building the railways from the coast to Kimberley or transporting goods there on waggons.

The railways eventually solved two of Kimberley's other problems, the needs for fuel and food. Of course, what were problems for Kimberley were opportunities for producers. The Griquas and the Batlhaping of the neighbourhood cut firewood eagerly in the early years of the diamond fields, turning what was already an arid region into a treeless desert in reckless pursuit of short-term income. On the other hand, the opening of a major new market for food provided opportunities for agriculturalists, particularly in Lesotho and the Eastern Cape, and peasant agriculture began to flourish, albeit temporarily.

The early years of Kimberley, as with all such mining boom towns, were chaotic and competitive. Some of those with lucrative claims, and a lot of luck, made money from the mining, but many of the serious fortunes were made by the diamond traders or those, like Cecil John Rhodes, who combined mining with other activities, in his case making ice and pumping the diggings dry. Out of this maelstrom there eventually developed a considerable concentration of capital. Rhodes, and no doubt others, recognised that the mines could be worked more efficiently as single units than as a multitude of claims, particularly as their depth increased, and that competition between the producers drove prices down and threatened to flood the market. All the same, it was only in 1889 that De Beers Consolidated Mines, Rhodes's company, acquired the monopoly over the four diamond pipes. From being seemingly anarchic, Kimberley had become a Company town.

Concurrent with this process, and clearly linked to it, was a change in the organisation of labour. The mineowners argued that their profits were being hit by the theft of diamonds by their workers, and their sale to unscrupulous merchants in the town, a practice known as Illicit Diamond Buying (IDB). They saw as the solution to this problem the housing of their workers in closed barracks, known as compounds, which they could only leave to go to work. Doing this also gave them a degree of control they did not previously have over their workers. Employers no longer had to fear that their workers would desert to others paying higher wages, and wages were therefore depressed. Labour discipline was also ensured. That the compounds were inhumane, overcrowded and unhealthy was not thought relevant. Logically, they should also have compounded their white workers, who were just as much engaged in IDB, but this proved politically impossible, even though strikes by white workers were defeated. Indeed, closing off African workers from the town was the source of considerable grievance among Kimberley's merchants, many of whom relied on African custom. Eventually, though, a compromise was reached, in which the privileged position, and higher wages, of the white artisans and overseers were preserved at the cost of the African labourers. Thus developed two characteristic features of South African society, namely the racial bifurcation of the industrial labour force and the housing of at least black migrant labourers in compounds.

The development of the diamond fields had the effect of unifying the labour markets of Southern Africa between regions, even as it intensified the distinction between skilled white labour and unskilled black labour. (The other two potential categories, unskilled white and skilled black labour, remained sources of conflict and uncertainty.) The availability of work in and around Kimberley and the willingness of Africans to walk hundreds of miles to engage themselves obviously influenced the composition of the labour market in other areas, even if

3.1 A Rotary washing machine, in early Kimberley.

in the event, in the Eastern Cape for instance, relatively few Africans availed themselves of the possibility Kimberley accorded. At the same time, the diversion of African labour away from Natal meant that more Indian labourers were brought in to work on the sugar plantations, although the first such immigrants had arrived in South Africa in the early 1860s. Equally, the demands of the diamond fields led to the major extension of South Africa's railway network, which had previously been limited to within a hundred kilometres of Cape Town. It was not yet complete, by any means, and transport was still slow and expensive over much of the country, but the region's mercantile integration was also proceeding apace. For the first time, Southern Africa was on the way to becoming a single economic sphere.

At the same time, the first attempts were made to create a single political sphere in the region. From 1875, South African politics were dominated by the attempts, launched by the British Colonial Secretary, Lord Carnarvon, to bring about the Confederation of the various South African colonies. Carnarvon was impelled to take this step by a number of border disputes between the colonies, notably between the British and the Orange Free State over the ownership of the Diamond Fields, and by displeasure at the hamhanded way with which Natal had handled the conflict with Langalibalele, one of the leading chiefs in the colony. More broadly, though, the Confederation policy was an ambitious

3.2 A Hindu procession through the streets of Durban. The
150,000 who arrived in Natal as indentured labourers were
joined by a much smaller number who came to the colony at
their own expense, as a natural extension of the Gujerati trading
diaspora which stretched through the western Indian Ocean. As
most of the indentured labourers decided to remain in South
Africa after their contracts ended, there soon emerged a large
Indian community centred on Durban. In some ways, they
recreated the divisions of the Indian sub-continent in the African
one. There were Hindus, Muslims and Parsees, of various

attempt to establish safer conditions for investment in land, labour recruitment and, more generally, 'the advance of civilisation in Africa and the general interests of the [British] Empire'. It turned out to be a total failure, primarily because the Orange Free State was in no way prepared to give up its sovereignty and most politicians in the Cape Colony believed it would only lead to the Cape bearing the cost of the new state, without enjoying concomitant benefits. It was, however, as part of the efforts to achieve Confederation that the British annexed much of what would be the Transkei, and later passed it over to the Cape.

In trying to push Confederation through, the British increased the level of conflict, and the degree of divisions, in the region, rather than decreasing them. This was clearest in the Transvaal. The South African Republic, although recognised by other colonial governments, in no way controlled the totality of its putative territory. This conflict of jurisdictions was particularly acute in the east and north. On the one hand, the Transvaal burghers were increasing their claims for land, even

3.2 (*cont.*)

varieties, and Tamil-, Telegu-, Hindi- and Gujerati-speakers, at least, among Durban's Indian community, and a consequent breadth of temples and mosques built. Equally they achieved a very wide range of economic position. There were those who managed to become relatively wealthy merchants, while the mass were poor with men and women working as peasant farmers in the sugar fields to the north of Durban, as petty artisans or as factory labourers. Against this, they were treated as a single entity by the whites, unaware of or unconcerned with the distinctions of Indian society. Indian political activism generally attempted to maintain this illusion, as a basis for strength and a following, while at the same time using the illusion of representativeness to promote a particular position within the Indian community. (There was nothing unusual in this: Afrikaner nationalists and many African politicians did much the same thing.) Early Indian politics was thus a matter for the trading elite, who brought over a young Gujerati lawyer, M.K. Gandhi, effectively on a retainer. However, Gandhi increasingly challenged the government in a radical, if non-violent, way, which was not in accord with the old elite's desire to maintain both its pre-eminence within the Indian community and its commercial advantages. Only around World War II would Indian politics, under the influence of a number of Communists and in alliance with the ANC, develop a radical agenda.

within the heartland of the Pedi polity, buoyed up in their expectation by the short-lived rush for gold, which had been found in the river beds around Pilgrim's Rest. They also were experiencing labour shortages, as the Africans moved away from their farms to the diamond fields, and had on occasion shanghaied labourers on their way south. On the other hand, the Pedi polity, now under the leadership of Sekhukhune, was growing in strength. Migrant labour, long practised, was now more lucrative, and the guns that made up part of the migrants' expenditures increased Pedi military strength. In addition, the pressure of the South African Republic on a variety of communities peripheral to the Pedi Kingdom made them turn to Sekhukhune for protection. The competition between the Republic and the Bapedi turned into war in 1876, during which the burgher army, assisted by Swazi forces, was unable to conquer the Pedi heartland and melted away, leaving the Transvaal state further in debt.

The Pedi defeat of the Republic served as an excuse for the British to pre-empt the agreement to Confederation and annex the Transvaal in 1877. There was initially no resistance, and the burghers appreciated the smashing of the Pedi polity by a combined British and Swazi force in November 1879. But, the elimination of the Pedi threat only increased the antagonism of the Transvaalers to their new rulers, by removing one of the advantages of the British presence. Nationalist dislike of British overrule could surface under the inspired leadership of Paul Kruger. The Transvaalers rose in revolt and shot to pieces the British forces sent against them. The British were not yet prepared to commit the full weight of Empire to regaining the region. Thus, in part for reasons internal to British politics and confident that they could exert sufficient pressure to ensure a degree of control when necessary, in 1881 the British recognised the resuscitated independence of the South African Republic.

The attempt to salvage Confederation by placating the Transvaalers had its costs, born not merely by the British, notably its soldiers, but above all by the Zulu Kingdom. Mpande may have come to the throne of Zululand with the help of the Europeans, but this did not make him the catspaw of Natal. During the 1840s and 1850s, he had slowly resuscitated the power of the Kingdom, a process which was continued by his son Cetshwayo after he had ensured his succession by winning a sharp civil war in Zululand in 1859. Mpande finally died in 1872 and, on his

3.3 Paul Kruger.

son's formal accession next year, the Natal government, in the person of the Secretary of Native Affairs, Theophilus Shepstone, asserted its paramountcy over Zululand, to a degree which the amaZulu in general, and Cetshwayo in particular, could not accept. Natal's assertion of claims formed part of a concerted attempt by at least some of the colony's inhabitants to extend their political and economic influence into its hinterland, which they saw as extending to the Zambezi at least. First, though, they would have to eliminate the Zulu kingdom, and they were provided with an opportunity to do so by a territorial dispute between the Zulu kingdom and the Transvaal to its west. By interpreting the legal resolution of this dispute in the favour of the Transvaalers and presenting Cetshwayo with an ultimatum with which he could not

3.4 This drawing, from the cover of the *Illustrated London News* for 10 May 1879, provides an idea both of the confused melees which occasionally occurred within the fighting of the Zulu war and of the savagery with which the British depicted their opponents.

comply, in 1879 the British High Commissioner, Sir Bartle Frere, who was desperately trying to hold Confederation together, triggered war between the Zulu kingdom and the British Empire.

The war began disastrously for the British with the destruction of a third of their forces at the Battle of Isandlwana. Once it creaked into full operation, however, the war machine of the British Empire was more than a match for any South African state. With only minor further setbacks – which admittedly included the death of the Prince Imperial, the last scion of the Napoleonic royal house, who had taken service with the British to gain experience – the British armies rolled through Zululand, burning its capital Ulundi and eventually capturing Cetshwayo, who was shipped off to exile in Britain.

Conquering Zululand was one thing; ruling it was something else. By 1880 the ambitious plans for extending British rule through Confederation were coming apart. With the central monarchy smashed, the British hoped to emasculate Zulu society further by dividing the country into thirteen autonomous chiefdoms, under twelve Zulu aristocrats and one Englishman, John Dunn, who had become an ambivalent subject of Cetshwayo's kingdom. The result was a sharpening of the conflict, long latent, between those rulers who attempted to maintain the old order of society and those who hoped to increase their wealth and power by expanding their trading relations with Natal or Delagoa Bay, often at the expense of their subjects. With the return of Cetshwayo from exile, tension gave way to civil war, which was only ended, after Cetshwayo had been killed, with part of the country being given to Transvaalers who had been brought in to fight and the rest declared a British colony. Between 1887 and 1897 British Zululand was a separate entity, and was then absorbed into Natal.

West of the Transvaal, too, the pressure of land-hungry Boer free-booters against African societies led to the incorporation of large areas into the British Empire. South of the Molopo river, whites, making claims on the basis of their participation in the wars they had fomented, appropriated most of the scarce irrigable land, and also stripped much of it of such woodland as it still possessed, for sale in the market of Kimberley. To the north of the river, in contrast, the Tswana rulers requested British protection while their lands were still more or less intact, a circumstance to which the Bechuanaland Protectorate, and thus the modern state of Botswana, owes its origin. The Basotho, in

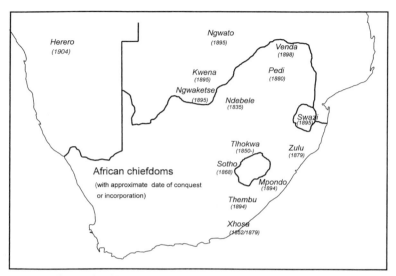

2 African chiefdoms

contrast, managed to achieve the takeover of Lesotho directly by the Imperial Government, thus nullifying its incorporation into the Cape Colony. This they did first by refusing to hand over the guns they had acquired, mainly by working on the diamond fields, and then by making the ensuing campaign so expensive for the Colony that it was only too glad to divest itself of the mountain kingdom.

Confederation had failed. The growing economic unity of the region had not been translated into political unity. However, during the years around 1880, the whole of what was to become South Africa was brought under colonial rule, except for a few small enclaves, notably Pondoland, which followed in the 1890s, and those areas of the Transvaal, notably Vendaland, which were formally white ruled but in fact uncontrolled by the Republic until 1898. Colonialism, if not on the terms the British had wanted, was now universally dominant.

In the mid-1880s, the rules of the political game changed, because the economics changed radically. In those years it was discovered that gold was present in the hills of the Southern Transvaal, in virtually unlimited quantities.

Once again, history had to work itself out within the confines provided by geology. Gold is widely distributed through a number of the strata which surface on the northern scarp of the range of hills known as the Witwatersrand, and dip away from there south towards the Vaal river. Within those strata, gold is found unevenly, but always at very low concentrations. Even in the richest sections, it is necessary to mine three tons of ore in order to obtain one ounce of gold (without taking account of those rocks without gold which have to be removed in order to get at the bearing ones). Most ore bodies, of course, are substantially poorer than this, or their working conditions were less favourable. Within these constraints, however, gold is available in what are, in effect, unlimited quantities.

The richest deposits of gold near the surface were found in the centre of the sixty-five-kilometre reef, as the exposure is known, in what very quickly after the discovery became the town of Johannesburg. The initial workings of the gold strata were on a small scale, as men hacked at the weathered rocks with pick and shovel. Even at the beginning, though, it was necessary to crush the rock mechanically in order to extract the gold, and soon it became clear that only in the ore from above 30 to 40 metres had the gold been weathered loose to be recoverable by amalgamation to mercury. Below that depth, the particles of metal were tied into the pyritic matrix, and could only be freed by a complicated chemical process involving considerable quantities of cyanide. At the same time, the logistics of extracting a very hard rock from deep under the earth, from where it had to be blasted loose with dynamite, were formidable. Consolidation was thus both advantageous and possible, as small claim-owners could not make their holdings pay in the new conditions, and could not ride out periods of depression. Within six years of the initial discovery, no more than eight conglomerates, or mining houses, each running several mines, controlled all the gold mining on the Witwatersrand. They were also sufficiently well capitalised to begin mining away from the outcrop, driving shafts into the rock to the south of main reef, in the justified assumption that they would meet the same geological formation some hundreds, and later thousands, of feet down. By 1893, they were able to produce over 40,000 kilograms of gold a year, and by 1898 nearly 120,000, more than a quarter of the world production at the time. These houses, of which the group of companies run by Julius Wernher, Alfred Beit and Friedrich Eckstein and known as the Corner House was the largest, thus dominated the economic life of Johannesburg and, in concentric circles radiating away from there, that of the Transvaal and Southern Africa as a whole.

Within a very few years of the opening of the Witwatersrand gold mines, the structural economic conditions within which they had to function had become apparent. Although it has a number of industrial and commercial uses, gold was, and is, primarily in demand as the guarantor of the capitalist world's monetary system. As a consequence, producers have little or no control over its price, and certainly there was no advantage to be gained, as was the case with diamonds, from forming cartels and monopolies to drive the price up. Mines could therefore only increase their profits by lowering their costs. And the largest such cost, and in some ways the most flexible, has always been labour.

The opening of the mines entailed an enormous increase in the demand for labour within Southern Africa. By 1892, there were over 25,000 black workers in the Witwatersrand Gold Mines and, with fluctuations, the number continued to grow. As at Kimberley, with which the gold mines competed for labour, the workers came from all parts of the sub-continent. At the same time, there was an influx of skilled miners from Europe. Both groups were drawn by the high wages, relatively speaking, paid in the gold mines, and were thus prepared to overlook the hazards that they faced, both from industrial accidents and from silicosis, a deadly disease of the lungs caused by rock dust, which, until controlled, killed vast numbers of the underground workers after a few years' work. In addition, at least for the blacks, housing, in brick and iron barracks, was rarely proof against the cold of a High Veld winter – Johannesburg is two thousand metres above sea level, and frosts occur there more nights a year than in London – and the incidence of pneumonia and tuberculosis was very high, especially as many workers arrived at the mines exhausted by the long march from their homes. Despite this, by 1895–7 the mines were beginning to force down the wages they paid to black workers, aided in this by the Transvaal state.

The subservience of black workers was increased by the impact of rinderpest. This cattle disease swept through Southern Africa in 1895–6, killing about 90 per cent of the region's cattle and probably as large a proportion of the big game and extending the zone of tsetse-fly infestation in the Limpopo valley, as the absence of grazers allowed the

3.5 Underground workers in New Heriot Mine, Johannesburg.

land to return to bush. In its wake, African societies, based as they were on the exchange of cattle for women through the bridewealth system, were heavily disrupted, and a series of localised millennial movements and other expressions of social disruption emerged, particularly in the Transkei.

By the mid-1890s, indeed, the South African Republic was beginning to recover from the shock which the sudden eruption of a massive and permanent mining city had imposed on what was still an agricultural society with a limited government. The problems were obviously enormous. A new city, with a population of over a hundred thousand, grew up as if overnight on what had been open grassland. Johannesburg was overwhelmingly male – among blacks between the ages of twenty-five and thirty-four, for instance, there was in 1898 one woman for every ninety-eight men. It was thus, in the context of the time, raucous, with much drunkenness and prostitution. It provided opportunities for gain in ways that were less licit than gold mining, such as running the prostitution rackets and so forth and preying on the miners moving away from the city with their earnings from a few months' or a year's work. At the same time, it was beginning to develop the polite society of the English-dominated elite of mine-owners and managers. Above all, it had to be fed, watered, cleaned and heated, and the raw materials without which mining could not function had to be brought in.

At the head of the South African Republic was Paul Kruger, who had been president ever since the re-establishment of independence in 1881. To prejudiced, progressive Britons in the late nineteenth century and since, Kruger looked and sounded like a living fossil. Certainly, he was theologically conservative, and relied for his support on landowners of the Transvaal's agricultural districts, for whom the Witwatersrand in general and the state-run distillery in particular provided a welcome market. He was capable of using his 'Boer' image for political effect, and was shrewd enough to recruit into the government a number of men with the administrative and legal skills he himself lacked. These were mainly Cape Dutch, notably Jan Smuts who returned from taking a law degree in Cambridge to become the State Attorney, or Netherlanders, who were instrumental in organising the railway line from the coast at Maputo (Lorenço Marques) in Southern Mozambique to the Witwatersrand. This was the shortest route, and had the advantage of passing through the coal fields at Witbank, but those driving railways up from the British colonies of the Cape and Natal were not appreciative of the privileges which the Nederlandsch-Zuid-Afrikaansche Spoorweg Maatschappij (Dutch South African railway company) received from the Transvaal state.

By the mid-1890s, the development of the state had led to two contradictory but nevertheless mutually reinforcing opinions among its opponents. On the one hand, there were those capitalists who believed, or at least purported to believe, that the Transvaal was too primitive and too prejudiced, in its present constitution, to provide for the requirements of the industry that was emerging. In particular, they objected to the exclusion of the *uitlanders*, those who were not burghers of the Republic, from the vote, and to the difficulty of acquiring citizenship. There is a sense, though, that, even though it was presented as what was then an acceptable racist denigration of all things 'boer', this sort of argument was little more than a complaint against the lack of influence that some capitalists could exercise on the Transvaal government. Thus, the Jameson raid, an attempted coup against the South African Republic in 1895, launched by Rhodes's minions at his instigation, and with the support of some, but not all, of the other leading mining magnates, was a backhanded compliment to the government. Some of its employees may have been corrupt in minor matters; the Republic itself was not for sale.

On the other hand, the development of the Republic was seen as a challenge to British hegemony in Southern Africa. The growth of the gold-mining industry had turned the political geography of the region inside out. In 1852–4 and again in 1881, control of the coasts was held to ensure control over the whole of South Africa; this assumption no longer held. In addition, the stakes had been raised enormously. From the early nineteenth century, the British presence in South Africa had been essentially defensive, predicated on the belief that it was necessary to hold the country's harbours to prevent some other European power threatening Britain's hold on the route to India. At mid-century, the Colonial Secretary, Earl Grey, had written that 'it would be far better for this country if British territory in South Africa were confined to Cape Town and Simon's Bay'. Around 1880, many leading Britons, though probably not Grey's successor, Lord Carnarvon, still held this opinion. After 1886, the Transvaal's position as the producer of a very large proportion of the world's premier strategic mineral, gold – and thus money – changed all that.

By the 1890s, at least some of those within the ruling elite of Great Britain were aware of the country's potential financial weakness. This was brought home to them by the crisis of one of the leading City of London banks, Baring's, in 1890, and expressed at the time by the then Chancellor of the Exchequer, George Goschen. Presumably the point was not lost on his erstwhile private secretary, Lord Milner, who was to become the Governor of the Cape Colony and British High

3.6 Cecil John Rhodes came to South Africa for his health, and then proceeded to make a fortune on the diamond fields, before entering politics where he became the Prime Minister of the Cape Colony. His stake in the Witwatersrand mines was initially relatively small, and his main interests came to lie to the north of South Africa, as his British South Africa Company colonised the countries now known as Zimbabwe and Zambia which during the colonial period were named after him. Completely unselfconsciously, he intertwined personal gain and idealistic British imperialism. His actions around the Jameson raid were thus driven simultaneously and without contradiction by a wish to create a Transvaal fit for capitalism, to extend British hegemony and to unload the costs of his northern adventure onto a united South Africa which would include what were then known as the Rhodesias.

Commissioner in South Africa in 1897. The regular bi-weekly ship-
ments of gold to London provided the assurance by which the City's
financial markets could maintain the supremacy of sterling (the British
currency) without building up large gold reserves in the vaults of the
Bank of England. British policy in the 1890s was not determined by a
crude desire to gain physical control of the gold mines. The British were
too sophisticated in the techniques of exerting influence informally to
need to do this. However, they did have a major interest in ensuring that
conditions for gold production were optimal and that the gold came to
the London market, and not for instance to that of Berlin.

In the late nineteenth century, British politicians could not have said
publicly that the goal of their policy was control over the gold fields and
gold production; they could probably not even have said it in private to
each other, and many would have rejected the thought if it had occurred
to them in such a concrete form. Rather their conscious, and proclaimed, aim was the preservation of British supremacy in South Africa
– whatever that might have meant, if it did not include control of the
gold fields. However, the idea that the Transvaal had to be governed in
a way acceptable to mining capitalists could be translated into terms
which were politically acceptable. As was noted above, the Transvaal,
and Johannesburg in particular, contained large numbers of Britons
(and other Europeans) known as the *uitlanders*, who were excluded
from political participation. If they received full political rights within
the South African Republic, then the government would be fully amenable to British interests. Furthermore, an end would be brought to what
was perceived as a scandal, namely discrimination against Britons.

This was a line of argumentation which squared very well with two
other prejudices to be found among the British elite, namely the belief
in the ultimate importance of race in political conflict – the British and
the Dutch being seen as races – and the notion that the conflict in South
Africa was between the British and the Boers. The British Prime
Minister, Lord Salisbury, had certainly heard such statements from men
he admired when he had visited South Africa as a young man. *Uitlander*
rights were thus an issue around which pressures on the South African
Republic from both capitalists and imperialists – in this context different people, though in alliance – could coalesce. The result was a steady
increase in the demands made by the British Empire, in the person of
Lord Milner, on the South African Republic until, finally, in 1899 Kruger

was faced with a choice between the dissolution of the state as it then existed and war with the British. The Transvaal, in alliance with the Orange Free State, chose war.

The war that followed has been known as the South African War, as the Boer War, or to Nationalist Afrikaners as the Second War of Liberation. It was by far the greatest military confrontation in the colonial conquest of Southern Africa, rather to the surprise of both participants. The Transvaalers had expected that the British would make terms as soon as they had lost a battalion or two, as had been the case in 1881. The British, in contrast, were confident that they could roll north into Pretoria within a couple of months. Both were disillusioned. The British lost several battles, but this only made them more determined to drive on. They could not permit the loss of international standing which failure to win would have entailed, and indeed the war was marked by the high point of imperialist fervour in Britain. Thus, slowly, the war machine cranked up, until by March 1900 there were 200,000 British troops in South Africa, there to conquer two Republics with a total white population (women and children included) of 300,000. And by the end of the war, a tenth of that population had died.

The war took so long, and was so expensive in men's lives and in materials, because some of the Boer generals, notably Koos De La Rey to the south of Kimberley and Louis Botha in northern Natal, exploited the defensive possibilities offered by what was then modern technology. Dug into the banks of the Modder river, the plains below the *kopje* of Magersfontein and the foothills of the Drakensberg on the Upper Thukela river, they could make use of the rapid fire of Mauser rifles and the concealment given by smokeless gunpowder to drive back British attacks. British generals were schooled in older forms of warfare, and had to learn in practice how to deal with circumstances not covered by their experience. Eventually, though, weight of numbers on the plains of the Free State and Northern Cape and an appreciation of the use of ground in Natal broke the Boer armies. In June 1900, nine months after the war had started the British captured Pretoria. Shortly before, Paul Kruger had left through Maputo for exile in the Netherlands.

The British had expected that this would end the war. They were wrong. For another two years, mounted Boer commandoes harried British communications, and raided deep into the Cape Colony. The

British reacted by looting and burning farms and crops across the High Veld, by building blockhouses to restrict Boer mobility and by rounding up all the Republican Afrikaners they could, shipping the men out of the country and holding the women and children in concentration camps, where thousands died of infectious disease. Half the white population of the Republics were either prisoners-of-war or in the camps, which were to form part of the justification for Afrikaner nationalism. But, by then, the unity of Afrikaner resistance had cracked. Those who came from landowner families held out longest, hoping to retain their privileges. Those who had been *bywoners* – tenants – were much more likely to surrender easily, or indeed to join the British forces, as the ties which had held them to the notables had disintegrated.

The decision of the Republics to surrender was in part driven by a recognition of the ultimate hopelessness of their position and of the suffering of their women and children. But there was more to it than that. The war had been fought under the assumption that it was between European powers. Within this, there was a place for Africans and coloureds as servants, baggage carriers, transport riders and so forth. Certainly in the Cape, there were many who exploited the needs of the British army, and the unreliability of Afrikaner wagoners and muleteers, to acquire a considerable if temporary prosperity. However, Africans were not supposed to be partisan in a white man's war. The British treated the Africans in the captured districts of the Transvaal and Free State more harshly than they treated the whites, and the Boers shot any armed blacks they encountered. Even deep in the Cape Colony, where the sympathy of the local Afrikaners was in general for the Republicans, on at least one famous occasion a coloured blacksmith thought to be spying for the British was lynched.

The Africans and coloureds saw matters differently. Almost without exception, they were highly pro-British. Even in the Eastern Cape, site of a century of wars with the British, the excesses of Republican policy towards Africans was sufficient to outweigh historical aversion to British colonial rule. Elsewhere, the Afrikaner dominance of the pre-war countryside, and the atrocities committed by some Boer commandoes, guaranteed the loyalty of coloureds, in particular, to the British Empire.

In the Transvaal, involvement in the war was more direct. Military action, in the strict sense, was rare, though one Boer commando was nearly wiped out by a Zulu attack. Rather, Africans used the destruction of the Transvaal armed forces to retake the land which had been but recently conquered and which they saw as their own. In the west, the Bakgatla removed all markers of property from the Pilansberg, and treated the area as tribal land. Stock was lifted in large quantities, sometimes on commission (which was generally not paid) for the British forces. Tenancy arrangements were negated. Men returning from war were given no access to what they thought of as their farms, and faced armed Africans ready to enforce this. Louis Botha, no less, Transvaal army commander and future Prime Minister of South Africa, was informed by the Africans on his Mpumalanga farm that he had 'no business' there, and 'had better leave'. The decision of the republican leaders, both military and political, to sue for peace was made against breakdown of social order as they had known it.

In 1902, after the Peace of Vereeniging, which ended the war, the British annexed the Republics, as the Transvaal and the Orange River Colonies. Though they were not united, a single man, the High Commissioner, Milner, had ultimate authority over all the four colonies, plus the protectorates of Basutoland, Bechuanaland and Swaziland – the last of which had made use of the war to evade a threatened incorporation into the Transvaal, while Bechuanaland had escaped partition between Zimbabwe and the Cape in the aftermath of the Jameson raid. The question was, what was the new South Africa to be.

Not for the last time in South African history, the answer was to be: in many respects, very much like the old. The British Empire had gone to war with the Afrikaner republics to re-establish and secure British pre-eminence in Southern Africa. Whatever else this may have entailed, it certainly did not mean the abrogation of property rights and of the supremacy of whites over the country's black majority. Where, as in much of the rural Transvaal, these had been endangered during the war, a considerable effort was made to restore them. In a carefully concerted campaign, blacks were disarmed, though they did receive some monetary compensation for their guns. Again, British administrations both in the Transvaal and in the Free State ensured that landowners regained power over their farms.

This was not an unambiguous procedure. First, the landowners had supported the Republican war effort longer than others, and were presumed to be those most opposed to the entrenchment of British supremacy. The administration did attempt to settle some English and English-South-African farmers in the former republics, but the numbers were so small as to have little effect. Secondly, their interventions brought the British into what was becoming one of the most contentious issues of South African society, namely those surrounding black landownership and the conditions of labour and tenancy.

During the era of the Republics, the great majority of land in the Transvaal and the Orange Free State had been parcelled out into white ownership. This was the property right that the British were protecting and restoring. However, those property rights had been exploited in quite distinct ways. The sheep runs of the southern Free State had long been a locus of capitalist farming, and in this sense were an extension of the karooid plains of the Cape Colony. Further north, land was held both by individuals and by large land companies. The latter were essentially waiting for the price of land to rise in order to achieve a speculative profit, and in the mean time were content to acquire income by letting land to African tenants, generally on the basis of a share-cropping agreement. Indeed, successful entrepreneurs such as Isaac Lewis and Sammy Marks appreciated that African families were the most efficient productive units on the High Veld, and ran the twenty-two farms of the Vereeniging estates, which straddled the Vaal to the south of Johannesburg, predominately, and successfully, as a large-scale share-cropping operation. Individual farmers often engaged in much the same sort of practice, as the markets which were increasingly available for agricultural produce in the towns of the Transvaal enabled them to accumulate the capital they needed to engage in agriculture on their own account from the share-croppers on the land they held by Republican title.

This was not a development greeted with enthusiasm by the political rulers of the Transvaal and Orange Free State, whether Republicans or their British successors. In both Republics, laws were introduced to limit the number of African families who might live on any single farm, in the hope of distributing African labour more equitably, as it was seen. However, these were not enforced, and the British government's furtherance of a commercial agriculture organised around farmers employing labourers also remained nugatory. They were even forced by the courts to grant Africans the right to purchase land and the period of Crown

A Civilized Native's Wedding Party.

3.7 An elite marriage probably in the Eastern Cape around 1870, showing the lengths to which respectable and affluent Africans would go to demonstrate their status and commitment to the values of white-led society.

Colony rule saw a significant increase in black landownership in the Transvaal – such as had previously existed had indeed always been held in trust by missions. The serious assault on black share-croppers and other improving peasants had to wait until after Union.

The commercial African peasantry of the northern provinces, as they were to become, were following much the same path as their equivalents in the Eastern Cape. There, too, the opening of new markets and a slow improvement in the transport facilities – although, as was pointed out long ago, railways were usually routed through white-owned land, and thus away from the concentrations of the African peasantry – had produced a steady increase in the number and prosperity of African commercial agriculturalists, generally growing maize, vegetables and other crops with the help of ox-drawn ploughs. The result was a much sharper degree of economic differentiation among the African population of the Ciskei and Transkei, between those who were able to benefit from these developments, and those who did not and generally saw the carrying capacity of their land deteriorating. An independent peasantry was also to be found in Natal, though probably in a smaller proportion than in the Eastern Cape. In both colonies this form of economic activity was particularly associated with those who had become Christians – known in Natal as the *amakholwa* and in the Eastern Cape disparagingly as the *amagqoboka* (those with a hole in the heart) – as was also the case in the north. In the Transvaal and Orange Free State, though, large numbers, among both the tenants and the townspeople, were joining the American Methodist Episcopalian Church (AMEC). This had been set up in South Africa by Afro-Americans, but was for a time out of the control of its founders. During the period, it was exhibiting a political and ecclesiastical radicalism which clashed with the aim towards respectability which both American and European missionaries considered integral to the process of conversion and, not entirely without reason, disquieted the rulers of the country.

Throughout the country, though, the years after the war provided increasing numbers of Africans with the opportunities to avoid working for whites. The measures for the restoration of class rule inherent on reconstruction had yet to bite, and even in the depressed market after the war there was a sufficient market for their agricultural produce. This partial withdrawal brought forth a sharp reaction on the part of the whites. It was in one sense heaviest in Natal, where in any event many

Africans considered mine labour to be more lucrative and attractive than working on the local farms. In an attempt to maximise African participation in the formal labour market, the Natal government instituted a poll tax. The disquiet this caused among Africans was exacerbated by a panic among the whites into the Bambatha rebellion, named after the leader of the Zulu rebels. Easily crushed as it was, this proved to be the last African armed resistance to colonial domination, at least in the tradition of the early colonial wars.

The same problems of labour shortage also afflicted the gold mines of the Witwatersrand. It might have been possible for the mines to employ large numbers of white men as unskilled labourers. Even before the war, there had been an influx of Afrikaners from the countryside into Johannesburg, and after 1902 the numbers increased, as the position of *bywoners* became ever more precarious. However, white wages were much higher than those paid to blacks, both because of the political pressure which white labourers could exert and because racial hierarchy could not survive the sight of white men exposed to the indignities and poverty which blacks were expected to endure. As a result, the one experiment with an all-white worked mine failed quickly, even though it was in fact geologically one of the most favourable on the reef.

The solution proposed by the mine-owners, in a moment of panic, was the importation of indentured labourers from China to work as unskilled labourers. In total, around 60,000 such men (and two women, one of whom went home immediately) were brought over between 1904 and 1907. However, this measure was not without some considerable cost. Within the mines themselves, agreements had to be struck with the white mineworkers before they would consent to the proposals. The result was, for the first time, a very clear division of labour between skilled and supervisory employees, who were to be exclusively white, and the mass of unskilled workers, who were either Chinese or African. This produced an entrenchment of the colour bar within the country's premier industry, one which was to outlast by far the immediate occasion for which it had been instituted.

The second cost was directly political. The British administration of the Transvaal was pledged to introduce some form of Representative Assembly to the new Colony within a few years. In their imperialist fashion, those surrounding Milner had hoped that they would be able to persuade sufficient immigrants to give the Transvaal a majority of

English among the male white population – presumed to be the only sort of people who mattered in electoral terms. (British women, admittedly, were greatly desired as immigrants, but mainly to prevent the men finding solace among the Afrikaners – or even worse the blacks – and thus not fulfilling their imperial mission.) However, the scandals surrounding the Chinese labour issue may have led to the diminution of the numbers of such immigrants, although the depression in the years after the war probably had more to do with this. More importantly, the controversies surrounding Chinese labour allowed *Het Volk*, a party led by the former Boer war generals Louis Botha and Jan Smuts – the Nelson Mandela and Thabo Mbeki of their day – to garner support on a populist programme.

The victory of *Het Volk* in the Transvaal elections of 1907 was in one sense a defeat for the British imperialist programme which had brought about the South African War and had informed the process of reconstruction. If British pre-eminence was to depend on the country being ruled by men of British descent to the exclusion of the Afrikaners, then it was not to happen. Never since has there been a head of government in South Africa whose first language was English. If, on the other hand, that pre-eminence was seen not in narrow racial terms, but as the construction of a social order in which British and other companies could operate in relative ease, in which the ideals of British society – which of course at this period included the subjugation of the Africans – were embodied and which would remain loyal to the British Empire, then the victory of *Het Volk* was a major step towards the entrenchment of that pre-eminence. This was demonstrated in the short term by the new Transvaal Government using troops to crush a strike of white mineworkers in 1907, although there was of course the ulterior motive of wanting to increase opportunities for Afrikaner employment in supervisory capacities in the mines. In the longer term, though, it can be seen in the conditions under which the four colonies came to form the Union of South Africa, some three years later.

The Union of South Africa was inaugurated on 31 May 1910, with Louis Botha as its first Prime Minister. Like all such voluntary subsumptions of sovereignty in a greater whole, it had to be preceded by much hard bargaining, most of which had taken place in the sessions of the National Convention held, successively, in Durban, Cape Town and

3.8 The delegates at the National Convention, 1908–9.

Bloemfontein between October 1908 and May 1909. In this, white male delegates from the four colonies (and three observers from Rhodesia, which it was hoped would eventually join the Union), all of them experienced politicians, found a set of compromises with which they were all minimally satisfied and which they could successfully defend in their respective parliaments. Once they had done so, the British Parliament too assented to the Bill establishing the new state.

In one sense, the political union was a recognition of the economic and social union which had already largely occurred. The trigger for the negotiations was disagreement over customs union between the various colonies, and it was confidently expected, not without justification, that political amalgamation would provide a valuable fillip for the South African economy. Moreover, Union could solve the contentious questions of the railway rates, a matter of great concern in a region whose economic heartland was literally on the watershed between the Indian and the Atlantic Oceans.

All the same, to reduce the demand for Union to the elemental level of economic calculation is to underestimate the feelings of a South African nationalism which were beginning to develop in the country. Once the immediate aftermath of the war had passed, those who advocated an English chauvinism, to the exclusion of the Afrikaners, converted to stressing a vision of nationality which was much more inclusive, though exclusively white and in its essence male. There were of course calculations behind this shift. Milnerite demographic engineering had failed to provide for a British majority in the country, even among the whites. A new Afrikaner nationalism was beginning to emerge among those classic ethnic entrepreneurs, the small-town teachers, lawyers and clergymen who were finding ways of explaining the defeat of the Republics in the war and were beginning to find publicists. To the extent that this was already seen as a threat, it had to be contained by the incorporation, as far as possible, of those who had emerged as the leaders of the Afrikaners. Many of the latter, for their part, were quite prepared to abandon the ethnic exclusivity of the Republics, both because they saw in Union and the imperial connection enhanced possibilities for economic progress, which would benefit their fellows as much as anyone, and because, having done their electoral sums, they realised they would never lose out completely if ethnic politics again became rampant. In this sense, 1910 was a replay, on a larger compass, of the politics of the Cape from 1852.

In the course of the convention, a number of compromises were made so that Union could be achieved. These included the clumsy solution for the new country's capital, with the executive and civil service based in Pretoria, in the old Transvaal, and Parliament sitting in Cape Town, over thirteen hundred kilometres away, with which South Africa has been saddled ever since. To make matters worse, the Appellate division of the Supreme Court, the highest legal authority in the land, was located in Bloemfontein, in the Free State. Only in this way could the competing claims of the two major colonies be reconciled.

A second major set of compromises concerned the franchise and the political incorporation of Africans and coloureds. The colonies had competing traditions. In the old Republics, only white men had been able to vote. The same had been effectively the case in Natal, although a few blacks had squeezed in under the most stringent of discriminatory rules – Indians had been excluded, no matter what their qualifications. The Cape in contrast had a system of economic qualification for the vote which meant that most white men (approximately 80 per cent in 1909) and a small proportion of coloured and African men (13 and 2.25 per cent, respectively) had the franchise. The number of African voters was kept down by the requirement that the landed property base for the franchise had to be held by individual tenure, thus eliminating

3.9 The Union Buildings, Pretoria.

those living on communal land in the Ciskei and Transkei, no matter how rich they might have been. There was no formal provision that Members of Parliament had to be white, but in practice this had always been the case. In a fair number of constituencies, particularly in the Eastern Cape, however, blacks were able to exert substantial influence on the results of the elections. Moreover, the franchise was seen, by both whites and blacks, as an incentive, a reward and a privilege.

The compromise that was reached at the convention was to maintain the existing franchises of the four colonies. This meant, of course, that only men were to be allowed to vote, although plans were made to facilitate the enfranchisement of white women, as a way of diluting the black vote. In addition, the rule that only white men could become Members of Parliament was formalised and provision was made for the appointment of a number of senators who were to represent the opinions of the Africans.

The preparations for Union along these lines brought forth a mass of protests from blacks. Particularly in the Cape Colony, the western-educated elite had been developing a style of agitation since at least the 1880s. Among the amaXhosa, such political action was seen as a replacement for the armed struggle which had failed to preserve their indepen-

dence. As the poet I.W.W. Citashe wrote: 'Your cattle are gone, my coun-
trymen! / Go rescue them! Go rescue them! / Leave the breechloader
alone/ and turn to the pen. / Take paper and ink, / for that is your shield
. . . Repair not to Hoho [the forest where Sandile the last independent
Ngqika chief was killed in 1878] / But fire with your pen.'* The white-
shirted, dark-suited, mission-educated amaXhosa and amaMfengu,
most of them voters for the Cape parliament, were hoping that their petitions, their political action and their evident respectability would safeguard and extend their political rights. These struggles were coordinated
through the rival newspapers, *Imvo Zabantsundu* and *Izwi Labantu*,
edited by John Tengu Jabavu and A.K. Soga, respectively, and funded by
competing white political parties. In the Western Cape, a similar process
had been initiated among the coloured elite, particularly with the emergence of the African Political Organisation, led by Dr A. Abdurrahman.

These men were joined in their actions by similar, if smaller, groups
from the other colonies, notably from among the *amakholwa* in Natal.
They went so far as to send a delegation to Britain, to petition
Parliament there against passing the South Africa Act which was to
establish Union. However, their actions had no effect. The British
government was much more concerned to reconcile the Afrikaners to
the Imperial connection than to address black grievances. It was more
than happy to treat South Africa as a white dominion, run, as were
Australia and Canada, by its own parliament with a Governor-General
representing the British crown. The opinions of blacks within the four
colonies were not thought important, although the British did lay down
stringent conditions, never met, for the incorporation of the protectorates of Basutoland, Bechuanaland and Swaziland into South Africa. It
was hoped, vainly, that the liberal traditions of the Cape would in time
be spread to the rest of the country. The Union was established over the
wishes of the majority of its population, as a relatively unitary state in
which the competencies of the various provinces were greatly limited.

* The translation is by A.C. Jordan.

4

Consolidation

The political union of the four colonies did not require, or entail, uniformity even among the whites. Rather, it provided the opportunity for latent conflicts to become manifest. The main arguments centred on the content of South African nationality. There were still those who had not accepted the verdict of the South African war incorporating the whole region into the British Empire. When this had definite consequences, with the outbreak of World War I, there were numerous Afrikaners who were appalled by Louis Botha's precipitate decision to enter the war. One general defected with some of his troops to German South West Africa, and a small group of Afrikaners in the Western Transvaal rose in a rebellion which was swiftly put down, though not before it had added to the mythology on which Afrikaner nationalism would feed. Thereafter, the Prime Minister, reverting to his old profession of general, led the South African conquest of South West Africa, which from 1915 was to be administered by the Union, initially more or less as a colonial territory.

The 1914 revolt was not really serious politics, and had no chance of short-term success. More threatening were the actions of J.B.M. Hertzog, an ex-judge and general of the Orange Free State. He was a member of the first Union cabinet, under the auspices of the South African Party, until he resigned in 1914 to form the National Party. The nation which this new party – and Hertzog after 1910 – claimed to be propagating was the white South African nation. This could however only be created if there was parity between the Dutch and English in terms of their access to power and resources. As this was certainly not

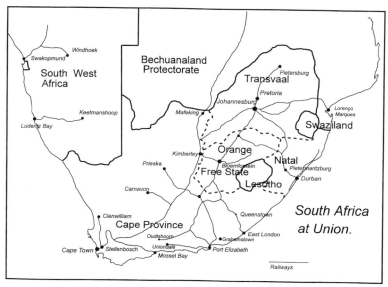

3 South Africa at Union

the case, the consequence of his position was a major push to improve
the status of Dutch within government business. Only in 1920 would
Dutch give way to Afrikaans as one of South Africa's official languages.
Nevertheless, the dividing line between Hertzog's South African nationalism and the burgeoning, more exclusive, Afrikaner nationalism was in
practice vague.

The corollary of white South African nationalism, whether Hertzog's
interventionist version or the variety propounded by Smuts, freer and
thus in its effect more English and more middle-class, was the exclusion
of the blacks from the body politic and their permanent subordination.
Between 1910 and the 1940s, this policy went under the appellation of
segregation. From the first years of Union, and indeed before, it was
clear to politically conscious Africans that, driven by the logic of white
politics, white South African governments would tend to erode such
rights as they had. The protection and enlargement of those rights
required a new form of political organisation.

In 1912, at a conference in Bloemfontein, the South African Native
National Congress was inaugurated, and John L. Dube, a leading Natal
educationalist, elected to the presidency – thirteen years later it would

4.1 The South African Native National Congress delegation to England, June, 1914. Back row: left to right, Rev. Walter Rubusana (Vice-President), Saul Msane; front row, left to right: Thomas Mapikela (Speaker), Rev. John Dube (President), Sol Plaatje (Secretary). This photo demonstrates the aura of respectability which the early SANNC was eager to present to white and British political opinion.

change its name to the African National Congress. As yet, it was not the organisation which could effectively challenge the development of segregation. It was from the beginning in the hands of the mission-educated Christian elite. A majority of its first council were ministers of the gospel. It remained in the tradition of petitions and delegations, largely ineffective, for several decades. However, its name referred to the Indian National Congress, the premier anti-colonial organisation in the world at that time, and one with which, through Gandhi, it had links. The SANNC's symbolic function as a national forum for African opinions was great. Eventually, its potential would be realised.

At Union, there were just under six million South Africans. Just over two-thirds of these were considered to be of full African descent, a fifth to be of full European descent, a fortieth to be Asians and rather under a tenth to be 'Coloureds'. It was a population which was growing steadily, at about 1.87 per cent per annum, so that it had nearly doubled by 1948. The proportion of Africans in the population was also growing, but very slowly. In 1948, it was less than a single percentage point higher than it had been at Union. In 1911, just over a fifth of the Africans were living in one of the Union's towns. Some 60 per cent of the half million men in employment in the towns were working in industry, with the gold mines as by far the largest employer. On the other hand, over 80 per cent of the 160,000 employed women (and one in eight of the men) were working as domestic servants.

These figures derive from the Census of the Union taken in 1911. The very fact that a census could be taken is an indication of the power of the new state. In principle, within a week following 7 May 1911, every household in the country was visited by government officials to note the names, ages, marital status, occupations and so forth of its residents. They will of course have missed a few, but probably under 5 per cent. Nevertheless, it was a considerable achievement to effect that degree of coverage. The organs of government could reach to the most remote areas of the country.

There are other indications of the extension of the physical infrastructure of the modern economy throughout the country. In 1910, there were, for instance, over 12,000 kilometres of railway line in the country, equivalent to about one kilometre for every 161 square kilometres of South Africa's ground surface. By 1933, this had grown to over 21,500 kilometres (or one for every 90 square kilometres). Modern roads began to increase in number rather later, as the number of cars and lorries only began to grow in the 1920s, increasing from 38,000 cars and just under 2,000 commercial vehicles in the early 1920s to over 400,000 cars and over 110,000 other vehicles by 1948. Or again, the number of post offices in the country in 1910 was 2,644, rising to about 3,200 in 1948. It seems reasonable to assume that at Union there would have been relatively few South Africans who were more than a day's walk from the nearest post office or from one of the 26,500 general dealers who took out licences a few years later.

In the major towns, the post offices and stores operated as part of the normal commercial services available in any larger population centre. In the countryside, and in particular in those areas where Africans held land, albeit under communal tenure, they formed a major link in the articulation of rural households with the national economy. Cash

entered areas such as the Transkei, Zululand, or Sekhukhuneland and
other parts of the Transvaal – or indeed much of the Protectorates or
Namibia – as money sent back from migrants working in the mines and
elsewhere in the towns, generally in the form of postal orders. It was
then often spent at the local trading store. The cash economy, the
demands of the government for taxes, the labour market and the infrastructure of communications held the country together. Segregation
was not designed to split it apart, merely to maintain its hierarchies.

The first attempted implementation of segregation was with regard to
the rural areas which had been alienated into farms for white ownership. The result was the Natives (now Black) Land Act of 1913, which
established the clear legal distinction between African Reserves and
white farming areas, delineated the two categories of land on the map
of South Africa and ordained that no land could be shifted from one
category to the other. This meant, in effect, that Africans could no
longer purchase land within white areas (or the reverse) – except in the
Cape Province, where the act was disallowed by the courts because it
made it impossible for blacks to acquire the wherewithal to become
voters. As a result, about 87 per cent of the country came to be considered white land, and initially only 7 per cent, increased to 13 per cent in
1926, the African Reserves. At the same time, the Act made illegal the
practice whereby blacks were able to make use of white land and to recompense the landowner in any form except labour. In other words,
share-cropping was outlawed.

  Like all legislation, the Land Act was an expression of the desires,
and in reverse of the fears, of its framers and supporters. Following a
decision of the courts in 1905 in favour of an American Methodist minister, the Rev. Edward Tsewu, Africans were able to buy and hold land
in their own name in the Transvaal. Furthermore, a share-cropper was
thought to look on the landowner as his equal, not as his master, a dangerous subversion of the hierarchies which the whites propagated. The
Land Act, however, could redefine all those blacks on white-owned land
as the farmer's servants, and thus subject to the discriminatory Master
and Servant legislation. Thus the Land Act was potentially the comple-
tion of the work of agrarian counter-revolution which regained control
of the countryside in the northern provinces for their owners following
the South African War.

(1)

(2)

(3)

4.2 Louis Botha and Jan Smuts (1), J.B.M. Hertzog (2),
Dr D.F. Malan (3).

The immediate result of the Land Act was an exodus of share-croppers from some of the districts in the northern Free State where it was immediately applied. Sol Plaatje, secretary-general of the SANNC, wrote some of the first, and still some of the finest, of South Africa's campaigning journalism describing the plight of the once prosperous peasants and their families evicted from their long-term farms into the cold of a High Veld winter. However, it took considerable suasion to induce white farmers even in the districts of the Free State that they should abandon their lucrative share-cropping relations with skilled black farmers. It was a racist vision that they were being asked to subsidise financially, and many did not. In time, a wave of violence unleashed by white vigilantes enforced social relations of inequality throughout the northern Free State. All the same, in the dry sand lands of the far south-west Transvaal, and no doubt elsewhere, share-cropping, with its premise of some degree of equality, lasted until well after World War II.

The impulse behind the Land Act and its vigorous extra-legal enforcement was not purely racist. It was also witness to a specific vision of the proper economic relations in South African agriculture as in the towns, which can best be described as capitalist. Throughout the 1910s and 1920s there was a steady rise in the value of agricultural production, outside the Reserves (and indeed within them), which makes clear that there was also a concomitant rise in the market for such products, both overseas and, primarily, internally. The government was propagating this growth by providing capital, through the Land Bank set up in 1912, to stimulate the development of agriculture along lines which it considered to be modern. Equally, more and more farmers had accumulated enough wealth in collaboration with their share-cropping tenants to be able to do without them. This entailed a steady increase in the degree of regimentation of the farms' workings by the landowner – or his manager – and in consequence a decrease in the autonomy of the labourers, both by the abolition of share-cropping and by a worsening of the terms under which they held land in exchange for labour. From being relatively independent operators they were being steadily degraded into a propertyless agricultural proletariate. It was, as a meeting later expressed it, virtually impossible for young men to acquire the wherewithal to pay *lobola* and thus set up as independent married heads of households. Their route to social maturity was being blocked off.

This did not go unchallenged. Labourers, like their fellows the world over, did all they could to counteract such a change in their status. This might be the surreptitious and anonymous cases of poison, with sheep dip, or burning wheat ricks. In the late 1920s, though, it developed into a major political movement which spread widely across the country, namely the ICU.

It is somewhat strange that the Industrial and Commercial Workers Union of Africa, which was founded by a Malawian, Clements Kadalie on the docks of Cape Town, should have found its greatest adherence among agricultural labourers. In so doing, it changed from its initial form as the would-be respectable Union which its white advisors wanted it to become. They might have respected the struggles of farm labourers on the wine farms of the Western Cape along the traditional lines of trade unionism, were it not that the leaders of this movement were Communists. They could certainly not appreciate the mass movement of tenants which the ICU became, particularly as it was very largely aimed against white rule in general. Indeed its appellation in Sesotho became *Keaubona* – 'I see you', more often 'I see you, white man!' Its great centres of support were in the Free State, the Southern Transvaal and Natal, where for a few years the generally educated leaders were able to mobilise a large number of the farm labourers in the hope that they would regain the land and the status which they, or their forebears, had lost. Its successes were few, although it was able to make use of the courts to redress a number of grievances. More generally, though, participation in ICU activities was likely to call down eviction notices from the landowners. Local conditions determined whether in a particular district the ICU was popular. In Umvoti to the north of Pietermaritzburg, for instance, farmers had transformed what had been tenant worked farms into wattle plantations, as new markets had opened for the bark used for tanning leather, and in the process had driven many families from the land they had worked for many generations. It is not surprising that the struggles in this area were probably the most bitter in the country.

Three further points need to be made about the ICU. First, for all its failures – and it petered out in defeat and division within a few years – it was the first movement to unite large numbers in virtually all parts of the country to fight local issues under a common national leadership. In the towns, in the white countryside and, as we shall see, in the

Reserves, hundreds of thousands of the red membership tickets were sold.

Secondly, the ideology of the movement as it came to be articulated in dozens of local movements was redolent with an appreciation of its continuity with the wars which had been fought against the colonisers a generation or two previously. Kadalie, indeed, was not trusted because he did not speak the languages of Shaka, Moshoeshoe or Hintsa, and it was generally believed that the ICU was struggling to regain the lands of the ancestors, who would give strength to the movement. Outside the Transkei, the millenarianism inherent in such ideas was not fully expressed. Equally, the movement was never united enough for the ethnic particularism which such ideas easily contained to become an issue. Nevertheless, both were clearly present as an undercurrent.

Thirdly, though, in at least part of Natal, the movements surrounding the ICU also led to a partial challenge of male domination within African society. One of the main local issues was the attempt by the authorities to ban the brewing and sale of *utshwala*, sorghum beer. Women controlled the brewing and kept the profits from the sales. In this way they hoped to increase both their control over male labourers and the sales of the municipal beer halls. This called forth a series of major demonstrations in 1929 in towns such as Weenen by women, many of whom were dressed as male Zulu warriors and carried fighting sticks. The women's anger was directed not just against government, but equally against their menfolk, who were seen to be wasting their earnings on beer, and not providing for their families. Thus, not for the last time, the eruption of social protest led not just to an attack on the formal political order but also to an attempted reconstruction of the social relations within what should not be seen as the undifferentiated mass of the oppressed.

By the time of Union, migrant labour had become an essential part of the economy of all the African Reserves of Southern Africa and of most households within them. In general, the only ones not deriving some income from migrancy were those where the male head of the household had retired from mine work and his sons had not yet reached the age to go out, or those of the rich, particularly the chiefs, whose wealth was based in part on subventions from the mass of migrant labourers and their families. Nevertheless, migrancy was restricted to only a small proportion of the population, that is to say to males between given ages. As a result, there was a continual tension between those who were earning and those who were not, that is to say between women and their menfolk and between elders and their juniors. In the early days, particularly in parts of the Transkei, migrants were held to their place of birth and the residence of their family by the payment of their wages in advance and in cattle. This practice was eventually outlawed. It gave too many incentives for workers to desert in mid-contract, and too much unrest when a man came home from a year's dangerous work on the mines to discover that his wages had died. However, it shows the efforts a man's seniors might go to in order to maintain his contacts with the rural base. They were, moreover, in broad terms successful. Migrant earnings were literally ploughed back into the agricultural economy of the Reserves, to the extent, for instance, that by 1930 there were nearly two and a half times as many cattle in the Transkei as a dozen years earlier, and three times as many sheep. In addition, the territory's maize yield reached its peak in 1925.

Relations between the sexes were more complicated, since the women in the countryside had had no authority over their husbands within pre-colonial society, and thus had no legitimated power to bring them back or to claim a portion of their earnings. Their influence was likely to derive from a man's need both to maintain a house and to have a plot of land worked in his home village if he was to be able to retire there. For as long as he acknowledged this, a man was required to pay something for his wife's subsistence. All the same, the man who went to town and never returned, leaving his wife and children in rural poverty, was, and is, a genuine figure in many South African families, and the town woman, who would trap the migrant, relieve him of his money and alienate him from his home, took on many of the attributes of a witch in the mythology of the countryside. (Such women, themselves, felt otherwise, as we shall see.) On the other hand, men who had married but were still engaged in migrant labour were concerned about the faithfulness of the wife they had left behind.

Out of this concatenation of tensions, there emerged the ideology of traditionalism in many of the rural areas of Southern Africa. It was not constant throughout the region. Both the precise pre-colonial foundations on which it was built and the particular circumstances with which it had to cope varied. Nevertheless, everywhere its core features included a reiteration of male supremacy within the household, a reformulation of ideas of masculinity with the dangers of migrant labour replacing those of warfare, and a refurbishment of the institution of chiefdomship. This alone could both hold rural society together in the absence of so many males and ensure that the women demonstrated what was seen as their proper subordination. Women, in these circumstances, had the choice between leaving for an uncertain life in the towns and acquiescing in their inferior role. Most chose the latter course, because it was the one to which they had grown up to be accustomed and because the ideology of neo-traditionalism required men to maintain links to the countryside, to remit much of their wages there and thus to allow their womenfolk to partake of the booty of migrant labour.

The ideologies of neo-traditionalism might be presented as a rejection of things European. Particularly in parts of the Transkei and Ciskei, there were many who refused to wear clothes of European style (as opposed to cloth of European manufacture), and still applied ochre as a cosmetic. From this, they acquired their appellation as the _amaqaba_ – the 'smeared people' or, in English, the Reds. Nevertheless, in their acceptance of the importance of chiefdomship, they accorded with the ideas of colonial rule in the Reserves which were being developed and propagated by the white South African state.

There had been attempts to introduce individual tenure in land into the Ciskei and parts of the Transkei under the Glen Grey Act of 1894. Even in these areas, Africans subverted the intention of the Act by considering that land was held by at least the minimal patrilineage, not by individual men. In general, both before and after Union, the thrust of so-called 'Native Policy' had been the maintenance of customary law, and hence communal tenure and chiefly authority. In the process, customary law and chiefly authority were redefined, or at least ossified, to ensure the continued social dominance of senior men and aristocrats. It was thus an accord with black neo-traditionalist ideologies and was a policy with long roots in the actions of all the pre-Union colonies, particularly perhaps in Natal – which indeed helped reconcile white Natalians to Union. Even in the Cape, indeed, the practice of government in the Transkei did not aim, in the short term, for the assimilation of Africans to Europeans, politically and socially, in the ways envisaged by the Cape constitution of 1853, many liberal missionaries and, above all, the mission-educated African elite. It was over their protests that in 1927 the government pushed through the Native Administration Act (retrospectively renamed the Black Administration Act) which formalised the role of chiefs and headmen within the local government of the Reserves, and for that matter dignified the Governor-General with the title 'Supreme Chief of all the natives of South Africa'.

These changes, the general incorporation of the Reserves into the nationality and a succession of droughts and stock diseases which struck at the productivity of African agriculture were not accepted without protest. The form that the protest took differed widely from district to district, but was generally mediated in various ways throughout the developing African cosmologies. Thus, in the heavily missionised Ciskei of around 1920, Enoch Mgijima was able to persuade a large number of followers that the only way to achieve salvation was to withdraw from a corrupt world and found a New Jerusalem. There were echoes in this of the Moravian ideals of the eighteenth century, which were brought down to him through the mission at Shiloh, near Wittlesea, and also of the Xhosa and Mfengu conceptions of pollution which had certainly not disappeared with the Great Disappointment of the Cattle-Killing. Once again, though, the millennium did not arrive, and the community he founded at Bulhoek panicked the government into dispersing it bloodily at the cost of two hundred lives. At the end of the 1920s, in the northern Transkei, the ICU too was interpreted in terms of purification and renewal, as the red ticket and the slaughtering of pigs would identify those who were to be saved from destruction when the black Americans landed in their airplanes – an image which drew both on the mission work of the AMEC and on ideas of liberation spread ultimately from the black American leader Marcus Garvey and popularised in the Transkei by Dr. Wellington Buthelezi.

With so many men away on migrant labour, though, it is perhaps not surprising that one of the most sustained local struggles of the 1920s, in the mountainous Herschel district on the borders of Lesotho and the Transkei, was carried very largely by the women. The poverty of the region in a decade of droughts meant that any interventions by the central government, in particular the registration of land, were forcefully opposed. The struggle was full of seeming contradictions. On the one hand, it made use of neo-traditionalist ideas of a return to a pristine African society and, in contact with Wellington Buthelezi, had its

4.3 Until the nineteenth century, the High Veld and the Karoo
had one of the greatest concentrations of mammalian fauna in
the world. Springbok in particular were present in massive
numbers, on occasion migrating in herds which must have
contained millions of animals. They, and other game, were the
target both of the organised hunts of the African chiefdoms and
of the depredations of Europeans whose horses and firearms
allowed some communities to live almost entirely on game meat
and some individuals to grow rich on the sale of ivory. The
British military caste, above all, came to consider the mass
slaughter of animals to be 'sport'. Extensive herds only survived
in the Kalahari and the tsetse-infested Mpumalanga low veld,
where the horsemen of this ecological apocalypse could not
penetrate. Elsewhere, the main wild animal was the jackal,
thriving on the colonists' sheep herds, despite a constant war
against it.

By the early twentieth century, then, game, once an almost free
good, had become scarce. Its slaughter was restricted to the rich
whites, as their sole mastery over the animals became a metonym
for their colonial mastery over the country. Africans who killed
for the pot, or for cash, were stigmatised as poachers. Tracts of
country where game still abounded were set aside, as National
Parks, for whites to view as tourists what they were no longer
allowed to shoot. The largest and most notable of these was
along the border with Mozambique, which became known as the
Kruger National Park. The wilderness was only achieved by

millenarian undertones. On the other, it was led by Christian women reacting against the poverty which made it impossible for them to buy seemly dresses, and castigated their menfolk for their cowardice. It had contacts with the ANC – not in this case the ICU – but developed a strategy of radicalism which did not sit easily with the conservatism which still characterised that body. Even though the individual economic power of adherents was small, collectively their consumer boycotts of local trading stores had considerable impact. Even in an area so distant from the centres of the country's economy, such weapons could work. It thus demonstrates again how far the common institutions of South African society had united the country.

The first Africans to live in towns in any numbers did so, naturally enough, in the Cape. From the middle of the nineteenth century, men, and a few women, came to work above all unloading the ships in Port Elizabeth, where for a long time the only way to land dryfooted through the surf was to be carried by an uMfengu, and in Cape Town. In Durban, too, there was early a community of African labourers, who were often employed in European households and gardens as well as in more strictly commercial positions. In both cases there was considerable scope for misunderstandings between the employer and the employee. In particular, the European ways of measuring time – in hours, in weeks, in months of arbitrary length, in years which included both the dry and the rainy season – differed from those of the Africans whose divisions of the passing of time were different, and more closely determined by astronomical phenomena.

In some towns, notably Durban and Port Elizabeth, Africans lived from the beginning in separate quarters of the town, which they built themselves according to their own architectures. In Cape Town, in contrast, Africans came to settle scattered through the city's poorer districts, except for the workers on the docks and railways who were regimented into barracks tied to their work. Towards the end of the

4.3 (*cont.*)
removing such African communities as lived within the area, and by dealing harshly with those who attempted to penetrate the area in search of food. It could be then set aside to allow tourists to take photographs such as this of a seemingly wild but not dangerous lion.

nineteenth century, however, Africans were increasingly driven out of those areas of the towns where they lived in close contact with whites, and forced to settle in separate, controlled townships on the outskirts of the cities. In Cape Town and elsewhere, the threat of plague brought whites to believe that Africans harboured diseases, and the residential segregation so characteristic of South African cities through the twentieth century was in the first instance a form of quarantine. In fact, of course, the slums which were created were themselves exceedingly unhealthy, and tuberculosis in particular spread rapidly. It was however largely confined to the poorest sections of the community, and thus no threat to those who made the laws.

At Union, the rules governing African settlement in the towns varied from province to province, indeed from town to town. In the Free State, for instance, Africans could not own or lease property, and had to reside either on their employer's plot or in municipal locations. In Johannesburg, in contrast, a few congested areas of African occupation had come into existence, notably Alexandra township and Sophiatown abutting the northern suburbs and a number of fetid yards in the centre of the city. In 1923, however, the Natives (Urban Areas) Act was passed which unified the regulations and also allowed for the possibility of clearing the slums. Intertwined with the technocratic justifications and provisions of the legislation, as was so often to be the case in South African political history, was a broader theory, namely the doctrine famously enunciated by Colonel C.F. Stallard that South Africa's towns were for the whites, and that blacks were only to be there in so far as they were 'ministering to the white man's needs'.

For the time being, the legislation only affected where Africans could live in the towns, and even then it took many years before it was fully implemented. As yet no attempts had been made to impose controls on the migration to the cities. There thus developed two main categories of Africans in the towns and cities of the country. The first was the migrant labourers, particularly but not exclusively in the mining compounds. In one sense, recruitment to the mines tied the sub-continent together. Individuals from, especially, the Transkei, Lesotho and Mozambique, but also from Botswana, Namibia and further to the north were sucked in by the great maw of the mining economy. At any one time in the 1920s, about 55 per cent of the approximately 180,000 black men working in the gold mines would be from outside the country, and most of the rest would be from the Transkei and Ciskei. On the other hand, for these men – and they were exclusively men – their work in the mines was an extension of their lives in the rural areas of the country, and beyond its borders. Mine work, and work for the whites in general, was seen by the amaXhosa, for instance, as 'grabbing', something quite different from the work required around the homestead. Nevertheless, the goal of that work was to sustain the rural base, to allow a man to be a fully adult patriarch despite the steady erosion of the conditions under which this ideal had developed.

The mine compounds were institutions designed for the production of wealth, and not for the harmonious social relations to which the men aspired. All the same, with great human creativity they created an order in which they could recognise the values which they had left behind them as they entered the land of the cannibals, as the Basotho called it, drawing on their folklore. In part this was predictable. The work of the mines was a struggle, against the dangers of the rocks, and the warrior tradition had little difficulty either in re-establishing in the compounds and underground the relations of authority which had once pertained on the battlefield, or in redefining manliness to exploit the new conditions. The Basotho, for instance, took great pride in their prowess as the only men able to dig new mine shafts, not merely to protect an economic niche. Other ways were more surprising. The sexual authority of adult men over women was recreated in the all-male compounds by redefining adolescent boys as females – shaven, well dressed, often with cloth to simulate breasts, receptive and submissive in bed. The youngsters knew that the mine 'marriages' so created would only last for a period in their lives, and could indeed utilise the gifts they received from their 'husbands' to supplement their income. In this way, they could all the sooner acquire the wherewithal to pay *lobola* in the countryside, and thus become adult, married men, both at home and during subsequent contracts on the mines.

The second category of Africans in the towns were those who had come to live more or less permanently in slums and locations away from the direct control of the Europeans, or in shacks or huts in their employers' backyards. By 1936, over half the Africans in the towns lived away from the compounds, just over three-fifths of them in family units. The provisions of the 1923 Act, banning all Africans to separate locations, could not be implemented until there was sufficient housing built to accommodate all the Africans in the cities. In the meantime, slums continued to exist in many cities, and in addition to work in the formal economy, both in secondary industry and services, including importantly household labour for whites, many blacks acquired an income outside the European dominated economy. Particularly for women, providing beer (and often sex) for the towns' majorities of African men was a major source of livelihood.

In many ways, the towns came to contain institutions which were evident continuations and transformations of pre-colonial or pre-industrial structures. In Cape Town, the legacy of slavery was still evident among the coloured artisanate, many of whom were Muslims. Among the Indians in Natal, too, while caste exclusiveness had not survived the processes of indenture, male dominance within the extended families slowly reasserted itself, having been somewhat diluted in the passage across the Indian Ocean.

Among the Africans, two patterns can be discerned. Particularly the men maintained contacts with their regions of origin. In East London, a predominantly Xhosa town, the meetings at a major strike among employees of the Railways and Harbours Board organised around one of the fractions into which the ICU had split were regaled with references to Hintsa and the other heroes of the Hundred Years War of resistance against the whites. This overrode 'Red' and 'School' divisions. Again, in many places, certainly both in Durban and on the Rand, young men working as house-servants formed themselves into regiments, fighting for territory, women and the loot from raiding the white economy. These bands, known as *amalaita*, were at once a continuation of pre-colonial forms of organisation and precursors of the gangs which have terrorised later South African cities.

The cities were not just places in which rural institutions could be recreated, albeit in transformation. They were also places in which the oppressions of rural society could be evaded. The *amalaita* perhaps had come to the towns to escape the domination of elders over their juniors. Certainly they did not recognise such authority while in town, and probably would have had difficulty reinserting themselves into rural society, should they have wished to do so. For many urbanising women, such considerations were much keener. From the end of the nineteenth century, if not earlier, there are many complaints made by adult men of how the women no longer respected them, and how they had gone to

4.4 Beer being brewed and food prepared in the open in Rooiyard, Johannesburg, photographed by Ellen Hellman in the 1930s.

town to live immoral lives. The issue even led to a minor revolt, in Lesotho in 1898. Turned round, these represent reactions to women grasping the opportunities provided by the new towns to increase their freedom. Most of those women who left the countryside had been married, and were either seeking husbands who had deserted them, or fleeing from an oppressive marriage, usually as a junior co-wife, or from the levirate after they had been widowed.

For these women, and indeed for most blacks in towns, life was not easy. To the stresses of poverty and of the uncertainty of a social system in the process of creation were those caused by the state, which raided the townships to seize and destroy illegal brews of beer. In these circumstances, individual misfortunes were common, and had to be explained and relieved. The old explanations in terms of witchcraft remained feasible, but were probably less attractive. They had flourished in a world dominated by kinship. In their place, at least in part, new forms of Christianity were developed, centred around the need to find ways to heal the afflictions of South African society. These were in particular the

4.5 Isaiah Shembe (c. 1867–1935), founder of *Isonto lamaNazaretha* (the Church of the Nazarites), here shown leading his male followers in a dance, was probably the greatest South African church leader of his generation. On the one hand, he was only one of a host of prophets who, taking their inspiration directly or indirectly from the Rev. P.L. le Roux, emissary of the Rev. J.A. Dowie of Zion City, Illinois, founded churches known, broadly, as Zionist. They have used the spiritual powers they have acquired to bring people to Christ above all through their ability to heal the sick. Most of the churches so founded are small, and often do not outlive their founding prophet, but one, the Zion Christian Church under the Lekganyane family of Sekhukhuneland has become one of the three or four largest churches in modern South Africa. On the other hand, Shembe attracted his Zulu followers in large numbers both because he was a genius as a hymnologist and discoverer of ritual and because he provided answers to the existential problems which the amaZulu of his generation faced as the old certainties of social organisation evaporated. His was a Christianity which did not accept the Western cultural epiphenomena propagated by the missionaries. For instance, it allowed polygamy. At Ekuphakameni (the elated place), in the hills north of Durban, he founded a Holy Place to which his followers repaired for the spiritual sustenance and solace needed to survive in the harsh world of white-ruled South Africa.

Zionist churches, centred around individual prophets with the God-given gift of curing the sick, especially those suffering from psychoso-matic illnesses. These churches were not, of course, confined to the towns. Indeed many of those with the most elaborated theologies were to be found in rural Zululand and Swaziland. Their greatest adherence, though, was to be found among the women of the African settlements of South Africa's cities.

Alongside the great extension of the healing churches was a general move towards all forms of Christianity. The mission churches continued to dominate African education. The new elite was also Christian, and fighting for respectability and recognition in a country which did not recognise what they saw as their rights. In the 1920s and 1930s, black elite politics particularly as represented by the ANC, was still deferen-tial. The churches had not taken up the political challenges of urban South Africa. Their greatest creativity as yet was in the *Manyano*s, women's praying groups which emerged in all the historic churches to provide solace and support for those struggling to maintain a Christian life for themselves and their daughters.

After the death of Louis Botha in 1919, leadership of the South African party, and with it the premiership, devolved on Jan Smuts, with Hertzog still leading the opposition Nationalists. The other major forces within white politics were the irredentist British of Natal and, more signifi-cantly, the Labour Party, which essentially represented the white working class of the Witwatersrand. In essence, there was not a great deal to separate the various parties, although of course their emphases were different. The Smuts government was responsible for introducing some of the major segregationist measures, notably the Natives (Urban Areas) Act of 1923. On the other hand, it was much less committed to the Afrikaner nationalist programme than its Hertzogian opponents, and much more responsive to the wishes of the mine-owners than the Labour Party would have wished.

This last attachment led to the government's involvement in the major crisis of white South Africa between the South African war and the 1980s, namely the strike in the gold mines in 1922 which came to be known as the Rand Revolt. This, like an earlier strike by black miners, occurred in a period of depression following the end of World War I. In economic terms, the strike came about because the mine-owners

4.6 Christianity allowed women to pray in public in a way which
had not been possible in the even more male-dominated pre-
colonial religions. Within the mission-derived churches, initially
the Wesleyans and later all the others, women's groups came
together and from the end of the last century were increasingly
formalised organisations. The *manyano*s, as they are known,
each had their own uniform. They provided fora in which
women could take comfort from each other in the trials of town
life, particularly in maintaining their purity and that of their
daughters and in providing sociability for people who eschewed
alcohol and its accompaniments. They allowed women to
express themselves, to preach, to pray and to find solace. They
have been criticised by those who think that church groups
should be more engaged, socially and politically, but they have
remained at the centre of African women's spiritual expression
of their Christianity.

attempted to reduce their costs by replacing whites by (much cheaper)
blacks in a variety of functions. It was thus not a conflict about wages
as such. The white artisans, both of British descent and Afrikaners, had
in general a standard of living which enabled them to maintain a family
in a small house, and even to employ a black servant. Rather it was
about job security, and thus the safeguarding of this standard. For this
reason, if for no other, it was a struggle in which the mineworkers' wives

participated with as much vigour, and indeed violence, as their menfolk.

In the event, the strike was crushed after the government had declared martial law and mobilised the army and militias. In total at least 150 people were killed during the revolt, and another four hanged after subsequent trials. It was however recognised that such clashes were, in the long term, to the disadvantage of all concerned. The period of confrontation gave way to a long compromise, to the mutual benefit of the mining companies, their white workers and the state itself, at the expense of the mass of black mineworkers.

In the aftermath of the Rand Revolt, the South African Party lost in the election of 1924 to the combined Nationalist and Labour parties, which formed the so-called Pact Government. J.B.M. Hertzog became Prime Minister, and was to remain as such until 1939. The main aim of the Pact was to protect 'civilised labour', that is to say those labourers whose standards of living conformed to European standards – in other words, whites. It was obviously a dual policy, at once aimed to protect those who already had such a standard and to raise to that standard those who should have. It could thus unite the representatives of the white workers with those who were attempting to promote the interests of Afrikaners forced out of the countryside by poverty, on the assumption that the improvement in their material conditions would be accompanied by an attachment to Afrikaner nationalism and its attendant institutions, particularly the churches. So could the Afrikaner nation be reborn.

The civilised labour policy and Afrikaner nationalism thus interlocked, but were not the same. The former could not be imposed on the mines without disrupting the compromises of 1922, but could use the state income generated by taxing the mines to promote the railways and building up the state-owned Iron and Steel Corporation (ISCOR) and Electricity Supply Commission (ESCOM), both of which had indeed been founded under the Smuts government, and had in H.J. van der Bijl a single chairman. Like the mines, these corporations had to find a compromise between the requirements of profitability and the pressure for a predominantly white – and for that matter predominantly Afrikaner – labour force.

In addition to attempts to use the state and its major economic enterprises to further Afrikaner economic advance, Afrikaner nationalists had from around 1913 been engaged in a two-stream approach to further the cause of the *volk*. One was economic. A major attempt was made, successfully, to coalesce small Afrikaner capital sums, much of which derived from the farming community in the Cape, into large conglomerates, the Suid-Afrikaanse Nasionale Lewensassuransie Maatskappy (SANLAM) and the Suid-Afrikaanse Nasionale Trust Maatskappy (SANTAM), which would invest and operate as a counterbalance to what was seen as English, or Jewish, capital. The second stream was cultural and political. The Nasionale Pers became a publisher of newspapers putting out a nationalist line. In 1918, the Broederbond was founded as a secret society dedicated to the furtherance of Christian National culture. Until the 1930s, however, this did not have the political agenda that would later make it so notorious.

In October 1929, the New York Stock Exchange crashed. This ushered in a decade of world-wide economic depression.

The consequences of the depression were felt throughout South Africa, but in differing ways in the various economic sectors. The first years were difficult for everyone. Commercial agriculture was hit hard by the fall in demand and thus in world market prices. On the other hand, the attempts of the British and American governments to stabilise their currencies by devaluing them led to a sharp increase in the price of gold, and thus to a growth in production, and in the value of that production, within South Africa. In 1940, 31 per cent more gold was refined than in 1930, and it realised, in pounds sterling, to which the currency was still tied, 160 per cent more than a decade earlier. The income deriving from mining diffused through the rest of the economy, leading to a long boom, which lasted from around 1934 through to the 1960s. After the kick-start given by the rise in the gold price during the 1930s, the outbreak of World War II was a further stimulus, both with the necessity of providing repair facilities for allied shipping and more generally because imports were constricted and because of the potential markets opened up by the presence of allied forces in the Middle East and South Asia.

The expansion of secondary industry benefited in the first place from ISCOR coming on stream in 1934, so that the supply of locally produced steel increased sharply. Small-scale engineering shops, metal working and foundries began to develop, particularly around the Witwatersrand where the major customers were to be found.

Employment in this sector quadrupled between the mid-1920s and the end of the war. More sophisticated operations, notably the production of machine tools, however, were not begun, and this remained one of the most vulnerable points in the South African economy. At the same time, there was a great rise in textile and clothing manufacture and, less pronounced, in the food and canning business. Total employment in manufacturing rose from about 120,000 in 1925–6 to about 380,000 at the end of the war, while net output rose from about 31 million pounds in the early 1930s to about 140 million a decade and a half later.

This expansion in secondary industry, with of course its spin-offs into the service sector, had considerable consequences for the social structure of South Africa's cities, and of the country as a whole. Certainly in the 1930s, a combination of a depressed commercial agriculture and a flourishing industrial sector led to the migration of large numbers of whites to the towns. In particular, young Afrikaner women came to work, generally for paltry wages, in the garment-working sector, as they were considered to have the sort of nimble hands suitable for this work. As they came to work alongside black men, this situation caused considerable concern among the white middle class, and the young women became the targets of sharp competition between the socialist labour unions and burgeoning Afrikaner nationalism.

While these whites generally had steady jobs, at least for a few years, the Africans who came to town usually did not. During the 1930s and 1940s, the turnover of African labour even in secondary industry was still very great. Employers apparently still felt no need to train their labourers beyond the requirements of unskilled work, and preferred the supposed docility of an anonymous and circulating workforce. The Africans were themselves in large majority first-generation townspeople. In 1936, for example, 90 per cent of those registered for work in Johannesburg came from outside the Witwatersrand. However, in comparison with the mineworkers, the men, and as we have seen especially the women, were much less likely to maintain contacts with their rural home. As it grew, from three-quarters of a million in 1921 to 1.4 million in 1936 (and 2.3 million by 1951), the black population of the towns was steadily becoming more permanently urbanised.

In some places, particularly in Port Elizabeth, municipal organised locations were built to house this steady stream during the 1930s. Elsewhere, many of the men lived for a while in single-sex hostels. As

4.7 The crowded and insanitary conditions of a mine-workers'
hostel.

soon as they could, though, they left these places for the townships.
Here those who could not acquire legal occupancy of a stand would
become sub-tenants, often in back-yard shacks, where the rents charged
by the established residents could be exorbitant. The alternative was to
move into the squatter camps on white-owned land on the periphery of
the urban Witwatersrand. By the end of the war these contained
perhaps a hundred thousand people, and still more camps were being
created.

The depression and the war dominated politics, both white and black.
By 1933, it was felt that the major economic decisions, particularly
whether South Africa should stay on the Gold Standard or follow Great
Britain off it, required a non-partisan government. As a result, a coali-
tion government of the National Party and the South African Party was
formed. Hertzog remained Prime Minister, and Smuts became his
deputy. A year later the two parties fused into the United South African
National Party.

In creating this new United Party, as it was always known, Hertzog
was able to carry with him the bulk of his supporters in the Transvaal
and Orange Free State, but not in the Cape. In 1934 eighteen Cape

members of Parliament withdrew into opposition, unable to reconcile themselves to cooperation with Smuts and what they saw as the forces of British imperialism. They formed the Purified National Party under the leadership of D.F. Malan, a sixty-year-old clergyman of the Dutch Reformed Church who had come into politics two decades earlier as the first editor of *De* (later *Die*) *Burger*, the Cape nationalist newspaper. Malan was a burly, short-sighted man who saw Afrikaner nationalism as ordained of God.

Afrikaner nationalism as it developed during the 1930s and 1940s had four main sources, which even during the long years of National Party government were never fully reconciled. The original basis of the Purified National Party was in the Cape, among the richer farmers and those behind SANTAM and SANLAM. They were using Afrikaner nationalism both to amalgamate Afrikaner savings and, eventually, to acquire state support for their enterprises. To this end, they became active within the Broederbond, which after 1934 took on an increasingly political and economic role.

The second main strand of nationalism was much more of a Transvaal affair. Only one Transvaal MP, the later Prime Minister J.G. Strijdom, followed Malan into opposition. As a result there were openings in the leadership of the party for a cohort of young intellectuals, many of whom had studied in Europe, either in Germany or in the Netherlands. One of the most influential of these men, Dr Nicolaas Diederichs, developed a vision of nationhood which was more all-encompassing than the Calvinist views of, for instance, Malan, as the nation came to stand between the individual and God. But Malan would not have objected to Diederichs's stress that the Afrikaners, unlike the English-speaking South Africans, were a *natie*, a *volk*. This was to be realised in part through the economic activities of newly established institutions for the salvation of the *volk*, out of the clutches of communist trade unions or the moral corruption of the cities. In this, there was of course room for conflict with the older economic organs of the *volk*, such as SANLAM. Against this, the work of culturally recreating the nation enjoyed wider support. In particular, the re-enactment of the Great Trek to celebrate its centenary in 1938 excited nationalist fervour as the ox-waggons rolled north from Cape Town to the newly erected Voortrekker monument outside Pretoria.

Thirdly, Afrikaner nationalism fed on a visceral hatred of the British empire and its activities. Thus, in September 1939 a majority in Parliament, led by Smuts, took the country into World War II over Hertzog's objections. Hertzog thereupon resigned, and with a number of fellows joined what was henceforth the Herenigde (Reunited) National Party. Out of respect for his standing he became its Parliamentary leader, but he was not trusted by the Broederbond, both because of his agnosticism and because he still stressed the need for equality between English and Afrikaans. Within a year he was worked out, to be replaced by Malan, and he died in 1942.

Fourthly, during the war, the populism of the poorer white Afrikaners in the urban centres of, particularly, the Transvaal found expression in the Ossewabrandwag (Ox-Waggon Sentinels or OB). Originally founded as a cultural organisation to maintain the spirit of Great Trek centenary celebrations, the OB acquired a membership of 300,000. During the war, it transformed into a militarist organisation following fascist and nazi models with its own uniforms, under the leadership of J.H.J. van Rensburg. A number of its members, including the later Prime Minister B.J. Vorster, were interned by the government for sabotaging the war effort. At the same time, the National Party heads forbade dual membership of the OB and the NP, in part because some of them considered that the OB was acting on principles antithetical to Calvinism and in part to consolidate their own position as the leaders of the *volk*. By the end of the war, the National Party had reasserted its position as the prime representatives of Afrikaner nationalism

By the late 1940s, too, Black politics had again become militant. This too had a variety of strains. The Native Trust and Land Act of 1936 had given the government powers to intervene directly in agricultural production, primarily to instill what were seen to be correct procedures and reduce the diminution of the soil through erosion. As was the case with enforced dipping of stock, rather earlier, these actions were often meaningless, occasionally actually harmful and always irksome. They lay at the heart of rural resistance which was to break out with greater militancy after 1950, as the powers began to be applied.

In the towns, in contrast, the 1940s saw the beginnings of the later explosion. The squatter camps provided ample opportunities for ambitious men who were able to provide protection and the elementary services which these settlements lacked. In exchange, they could enrich themselves at the expense of the residents, and men such as James Mpanza in the Sofasonke settlement outside Johannesburg became the archetypes of the township warlords of later years, running a protection racket, but at the same time offering some genuine protection and representation for grievances. In the more established locations, in contrast, there was both the organic development of court structures which mirrored the *kgotla*s and other institutions of African societies, and the emergence of a community-based politics of protest against the imposition of the structures of segregation.

In at least two cases, in the bus boycotts of Alexandra in Johannesburg and at Brakpan in the East Rand, the leadership of such protests was linked to national political parties. The most prominent figures, Gaur Radebe, a lawyer's clerk, and David Bopane, a teacher brought up in Sekhukhuneland, respectively, were from the early 1940s members of both the Communist Party of South Africa and the ANC. The Party had been founded in 1920 as an attempt to unite a variety of small socialist groupings among the white working class. While initially it had engaged in a certain amount of trade union work among the Africans and coloureds, during most of the 1920s and 1930s it dissipated its energy in the internal struggles characteristic of so many sects. Loyalty to Moscow was the prime value and the Party was above all concerned to root out heresy in its own ranks, with the Comintern acting as the Inquisition. It was only after 1936, when a new Central Committee was formed and the headquarters moved to Cape Town, that the party began to regain any dynamism.

It is somewhat ironic that a party whose rationale was to work among the working class should gain strength by relocating away from the Witwatersrand, where its natural constituency was to be found. Nevertheless, with the internal struggles at least temporarily in abeyance, party members could engage in broader political work, both in the various African communities and by building up on trade union work. Much of the most successful work in the 1930s was among women, both the Afrikaner seamstresses in the garment industry of the Witwatersrand and the largely coloured workers in the food and canning industry in the South-West Cape. However, the most spectacular interventions came when the Party began to make contact with the gold miners, resulting in a major mine-workers' strike in August 1946.

At its peak, the strike brought out between sixty and seventy thousand mineworkers under the auspices of the African Mine Workers Union, demanding a wage increase and better food. The strike was smashed, with the help of state, at the cost of twelve dead. The Union itself then collapsed. Nevertheless, such a mobilisation, representing a very high proportion of the mineworkers, was achieved because of the effective utilisation by the Union of the traditions of leadership and defiance within the mine compounds. The key figure was J.B. Marks, the son of a white railway worker from Ventersdorp and an African mother. He was a long-time Communist who had been briefly expelled from the party in 1937, but would end his life as its general secretary. He appreciated how the 'old tribal organizations', as he called them, would respond very well to the basic message of collective bargaining and action. He was able to work through the room representative in the various compounds, even though he probably did not understand the extent to which they had been democratically chosen and acted to protect the rights acquired over the years by the mineworkers. It would not be the last time that political activists made use, almost inadvertently, of values and traditions of organisation whose full import they did not grasp.

The resuscitation of the Communist Party was paralleled by that of the African National Congress, although the relation between the two was not entirely comfortable. By the 1940s, a cohort of young men were becoming disillusioned with the politeness and moderation of the ANC's leadership, believing, correctly, that the Joint Councils of Africans and liberal Europeans would produce no improvement in African political rights, and indeed could not even prevent their deterioration. Many of these men had been, or were, studying at the University of Fort Hare, which had grown out of a mission-run secondary school to be the only institution of higher learning open to African students. Their intellectual leader, however, was Anton Lembede, who was a largely self-educated son of a Zulu farm worker and a devout Catholic. He had come to work in Johannesburg, but hated the moral degeneration, as he saw it, of city life. He distrusted the Communists, and more generally argued that liberation, which had to be psychological as much as political, could not come through institutions in which Africans were *de facto* subordinate to Europeans.

It remained a question as to how far Lembede's nationalism would be accepted within the ANC, that is to say to what extent that body should simply be the representative of the nation or to what extent nationalism should be exclusively African. As yet, though, this difference of opinion was not crucial. In 1944, Lembede as ideologue joined forces with others who were more pragmatic in their approach, notably A.P. Mda, to form the Youth League within the ANC, open to all those between the ages of twelve and forty. Among the founder members was Nelson Rohihlahla Mandela, who had come to Johannesburg to train as a lawyer after being expelled from Fort Hare. The Youth League saw its task as that of revitalising a fairly moribund institution and turning it into a mass party of protest. After 1948, when the National Party under Dr Malan won the white elections and took power within the country, this would be more than ever necessary.

5

Apartheid

On 26 May 1948, white South Africa went to the polls. The result, rather to everyone's surprise, was a victory for the National Party under Dr D.F. Malan, in alliance with the Afrikaner Party of N.C. Havenga, which was essentially those who remained faithful to Hertzog's legacy. Between them they won seventy-nine seats in the new Parliament, as opposed to sixty-five for the United Party and six for the Labour Party. Considering that before the election the United Party had held eighty-nine seats and the Nationalists forty-eight, this represented a considerable turnaround. Smuts, who had himself been defeated in the constituency of Standerton, retired, and died, aged eighty, two years later. The National Party was to remain in power for a month under forty-six years.

To explain this result, two points have to be made. First, the election was extremely close, and its outcome in part the product of the electoral system. Given the constituency system then in force, if only ninety-one people out of over a million, strategically placed, had voted the other way, then the United party would have won four more seats and hung the Parliament – and might even have been able to govern with the help of the three white representatives of the Africans. Indeed the National party only received 41.5 per cent of the votes cast. In part, admittedly, this was because it did not contest all constituencies, but even had it done so it would probably not have increased its share of the vote by more than a couple of percentage points. The Nationalists benefited greatly from the ruling that rural seats need have fewer voters than the urban ones. Also, they won many seats by tiny majorities, while the

UP piled up superfluous votes in places where they were already sure of success.

Secondly, though, the election results reflected the success of the National Party machine, far superior to that of the UP, and also a clear shift in political opinion, both nationally and, most importantly, among two key groups of voters. In general terms, the resuscitation of Afrikaner nationalism and distrust of J.H. Hofmeyr, the pug-faced ex-child prodigy who was expected to be Smuts's successor, swung a significant proportion of voters towards the National Party. More specifically, the maize farmers of the Transvaal had found difficulty in keeping hold of their black labour in face of competition from the burgeoning industry of the Witwatersrand, which inclined them towards the National Party, while those who had had a residual loyalty to the Party of Botha and Smuts ever since the South African War were becoming ever fewer in number as the years passed. Again, after years of hard ideological and organisational work, the Afrikaner working class of the Witwatersrand came into the nationalist fold. The nationalist capture of the Mine Workers Union in 1947, following a hard strike of white workers, symbolised this achievement ahead of the election. And it was the swing of the rural Transvaal and a number of the urban seats, notably on the Witwatersrand and in Pretoria, which put the National Party into power.

The election was won under the slogan 'apartheid' – literally 'separateness' – which was to become the watchword of the government and a world-wide term of abuse among its opponents. Malan's party did not come into office, however, with a fully operationalised programme of action. Two matters were clear, and were addressed in the first years after 1948. The Government's first priority was to assure continuing in office. To this end, whites in the mandated territory of South West Africa, German- and Afrikaans-speakers who could be expected to support the NP, were enfranchised, which provided the Party with six extra seats. On the other hand, a long and constitutionally messy process was initiated to remove the coloureds in the Cape Province from the common role, as they were seen as swinging a number of seats towards the United Party. Together with a certain amount of gerrymandering, and the continued rural bias, National Party rule was never in doubt electorally, even though it would be another three elections before the Nationalists received majority support among the white electorate.

Secondly, whatever apartheid meant, and this was not yet clear, it certainly entailed the recognition and separation of specific groups of people. The criteria by which these were demarcated were not racist, at least in the formal sense of the word. There was of course an undertone of intense racism within apartheid, but in strict theory, the National Party ideologues always emphasised the importance of ethnicity, seeing the various nations of South Africa as God-created entities, on the model of their own self-image of Afrikanerdom. These had to be preserved in all their purity. The state took it upon itself to do this, both by assigning everyone to one of the national categories within South Africa, through the Population Registration Act of 1950, and, in theory, freezing these categories for all time through the Mixed Marriages Act of 1949 and the Immorality Act – which despite its title was only concerned with the immorality of heterosexual intercourse across the colour line – of 1950. The consequences of these measures in individual suffering were on occasion very great. Families could be broken up and relatives assigned to, or making claims to, different racial statuses were divided. Many court cases for 'reclassification' were begun. Such suffering was subservient to the order the National Party wished to impose on the land. In part as a continuation of this and in part in reaction to international trends of the early years of the Cold War, the government also acted against the Communist Party and a host of other organisations rightly or wrongly seen as furthering its aims, passing the Suppression of Communism Act in 1950.

In the more socio-economic interpretation of the slogan of apartheid, opinions were more divided. This was especially so with regard the urbanisation of Africans. Indeed, the whole development of apartheid, and its eventual demise, can be seen as driven by attempts to control the numbers and behaviour of Africans within South Africa's cities, and by the resistance to such control by the victims of such policies. What went on in the Reserves, and in particular the measures to foist independence on what had become known as the Bantustans, were in an important sense a consequence of government actions and policies towards the cities.

The National Party went into the elections of 1948 with (at least) two contradictory visions of apartheid within its programmatic documents. On the one hand there were those visionaries who hoped to bring about a full dissociation between whites and Africans, in other words to brake

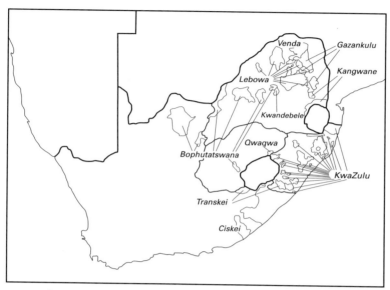

4 Bantustans

and reverse the process whereby South Africa had become an economically integrated country. Migrant labour for the mines, corralled in the compounds, might be allowed, but for the rest it was believed that in the long term white power could not survive the overwhelming weight of African numbers. It would be a long and difficult process to undo the interdependence which had built up over the generations, but eventually increased mechanisation and the greater use of white labour would enable the whites to do without African labour. On the other hand, the farmers of the Transvaal had switched to the National Party in order to be assured of black labour, and were not going to forego that reward, nor were the industrialists, particularly those who had set up recently with the aid of Afrikaner capital, willing to risk their businesses for some future white Utopia. What they wanted from government was a black labour force which was disciplined and cheap.

The task of reconciling and moving beyond these contradictions fell to Dr Hendrik Verwoerd. Born in the Netherlands in 1902, he had arrived in South Africa two years later. After schooling in Zimbabwe and the Free State, he had gone to Stellenbosch University, where he had

5.1 Dr H.F. Verwoerd

had a glittering career as a psychologist and philosopher, becoming a professor at the age of twenty-six. In 1936, he had quit academic life to become the editor of *Die Transvaaler*, in which capacity he had both revitalised the Transvaal National Party and proved an implacable enemy of the *Ossewabrandwag*, which he saw as splitting Afrikanerdom, and no doubt as athwart his own ambitions. In 1948, he was defeated in the Parliamentary elections, but was appointed to the Senate, and in 1950 was made Minister of Native Affairs. A man of domineering intellect, he was contemptuous of fools and opponents, categories he tended to conflate.

At the Native Affairs Department, Verwoerd attempted to solve the problems inherent in the demands of apartheid through the Urban

Labour Preference Policy. The idea of this was that no Africans would be allowed to come to work in the towns until all those who were already there had been absorbed by the white labour market. In order to administer this, a whole massive bureaucracy of labour bureaux was set up, charged with distributing Africans between the various firms in the towns. Furthermore, the movement of Africans between parts of South Africa was heavily restricted and controlled. The cynically entitled Abolition of Passes and Documents Act of 1952 required all Africans to carry a 'reference book' – a pass by any other name – which noted their employment history and residence rights. Together with the Native Laws Amendment Act of the same year, this accepted that there were certain Africans who were permanently urbanised, and who were thus granted rights of permanent residence in the cities. To qualify for these, the notorious Section 10 rights, a man had to have been born in the town or to have worked continuously for the same employer for ten years, or for different employers for fifteen. An artificial category, later known as 'the insiders', was therefore created, but the status could not be transferred to another municipality. Women could also acquire the same rights by marriage to a man who had them, and until the late 1950s women were generally not compelled to take out reference books. Contrary to their intentions, then, the Acts did in practice allow a steady trickle of Africans into permanent residence in the cities, through leakages in the dam, as it were.

There were two other major drives associated with this policy during the 1950s. The first was about urban space. In a number of towns there were enclaves where Africans had managed to acquire, and to hold on to, landed property, where they lived as in suburbs, away from the control of state officials. The most notable of these was Sophiatown, seven kilometres to the north-west of Johannesburg's city centre. This became a major target, in part because the Communist Party was strongly represented there, and in general because it was the kernel of Johannesburg's black cultural life. The government's attack, which led to the clearance of the area in the course of 1956 and the eviction of the residents to new townships in what was becoming Soweto, was presented as slum clearance. As Sophiatown was hardly a slum, and many other areas which were temporarily left alone were far worse, these actions were in fact more a move against political opponents. This was driven home after the area had been razed by the National Party govern-

5.2 More obviously than most other facets of South African life, its finest music has come out of the development of African forms in and in reaction to the new world of its cities. Two main strands can be discerned. One, known as *isicathamiya*, is sung *a cappella* by male choirs, of which the most famous, both in the country and internationally, has been Ladysmith Black Mambazo. It is a Zulu style, articulating the world of the country in the city, and *vice versa*, and was much influenced at its formation both by the forms of Zulu wedding songs and by the minstrel groups from the United States which toured South Africa at the end of the last century.

The other main style is the jazz which evolved above all on the Witwatersrand, again heavily influenced by the hearing of American records. Its early evolution came from the development of, on the one hand, elite vaudeville groups and, on the other, the *marabi* style played on the piano in the shebeens of the slumyards, and often accompanied by sexually explicit *famo* women's dancing. In the 1940s and 1950s, particularly in Sophiatown, these came together to create the mature jazz known as *mbaqanga*. From this milieu, a number of renowned performers emerged, notably the alto-saxophonist Kippy Moeketsi (shown here playing the clarinet with the Jazz Dazzlers in the 1950s), the vocalist Miriam Makeba, the trumpeter Hugh Masekela and the pianist Dollar Brand (Abdullah Ibrahim), the last three of whom went into exile in the ment naming the white suburb built on its site as Triomf (Triumph). For the time being they had won.

The second drive had to do with Black education. The developments here were ambivalent. Before 1948, black education had been almost exclusively in the hands of the missions, although the government paid teachers' salaries. A few of the schools were of the highest class, as was the University of Fort Hare to which a fortunate few could aspire. Against this, the numbers involved at the peak of education were minuscule. In 1949, for instance, there were no more than 284 African students, out of 343 in total, at Fort Hare, and no more than half as many scattered through the country's other universities. In general, Black education was underfunded. The mass of black schools were thoroughly ramshackle, and in any case only catered for a small proportion of potential pupils. Approximately 30 per cent of children between the ages of seven and sixteen attended school in 1949, for instance.

The Verwoerdian initiative promoting what became known as Bantu education had a double effect. On the one hand, it brought African education firmly under the control of the state. The school system was consciously used to spread the messages of apartheid. The ethos pervading educational policy, at least outside the Reserves, was that African education should be limited to those skills valuable for the maintenance of the white run economy, and the emphasis was on the basic skills learnt in the first four years at school. On the other hand, the number of those who participated in education – enjoyed is surely the wrong word here – increased very substantially. In a few areas of South Africa, notably parts of the highly missionised Eastern Cape, the levels of literacy had been very high, perhaps eighty per cent, and diminished considerably after the introduction of Bantu education. In general, though, an ever greater proportion of Africans acquired some degree of literacy and numeracy, and surprisingly large numbers went on to secondary school and, after the foundation of specifically Black universities, to higher education as well. By the mid-1980s, after four decades of apartheid,

5.2 (*cont.*)
early 1960s. For a brief moment in the 1950s, this jazz was associated with the black writers associated with *Drum Magazine*, including Henry Nkhumalo, Todd Matshikiza, Lewis Nkosi and Es'kia Mphahlele, in a short flowering of literary and musical creativity.

the number of black university students was sixty times that of the later 1940s, (ninety times if those studying by correspondence at the University of South Africa are included), and over the country as a whole the proportion of African children attending school is estimated to have risen to 50 per cent in 1976, and probably to 85 per cent by the early 1990s. What this all meant in terms of functional literacy is difficult to say. In 1995, 80 per cent of black adults – and 40 per cent of whites – failed a test of functional literacy and numeracy, at a level more or less equivalent to seven years of schooling, which meant that about half of those, both black and white, who had completed such schooling had lost the skills supposedly acquired there.

The Urban Labour Preference Policy was in general not appreciated by employers, above all those who relied on cheap, unskilled labour. Africans with Section 10 rights were generally seen as more politicised and less pliable, and the constriction of the market allowed them to demand higher wages. Indeed, even some of those institutions which might be seen as most susceptible to government pressure, including the municipality of Pretoria, the state capital, continued to rely on migrants to perform their unskilled tasks.

The objections of such employers were, of course, as nothing compared to the protests which the introduction of the various apartheid measures engendered among the African population. The ANC, reinvigorated by the foundation of the Youth League in the 1940s, now had issues enough around which to agitate. Much of its work in this was aided by individuals, both black and white, who were members of the South African Communist Party, an underground organisation which had been formed in 1953 to include the more active members of the old CPSA, which had disbanded following the Suppression of Communism Act. While the ANC was still only open to Africans, its non-African sympathisers, many of whom were Communists, could become members of the South African Indian Congress, the Coloured Peoples Congress and the (white) South African Congress of Democrats, which together made up what was known as the Congress Alliance.

In national terms, the major campaign which the ANC launched was in defiance of the unjust laws, as they termed them, which had been introduced by the National Party. The campaign itself began in the winter of 1952, in continuation of and under the inspiration of massive meetings of protest which had been held in celebration of the tercente-

5.3 Albert Luthuli, president of the ANC.

nary of Van Riebeeck's landing in April of that year. The campaign itself was of an almost religious character. The influence of Gandhi's ideas of self-sacrifice as a way to political success was very evident. Selected men and women gave themselves up to political martyrdom, by ostentatiously breaking the laws, and they were often accompanied by religious meetings, including the presence of *Manyano*s in their uniforms.

While the defiance campaign was putatively national, organised from the Transvaal with Nelson Mandela as volunteer in chief, in fact its impact in the various parts of the country was very diffuse. Just over 71 per cent of all arrests were made in the Eastern Cape, and over 31 per cent were in the towns of Port Elizabeth and its close neighbour Uitenhage. There were good reasons for this. The area had a long tradition of militancy, reaching back into the wars of resistance in the nineteenth century. Its African population still had some rights from its Cape colonial past, which were being eroded. It was also desperately poor, even by South African standards. The African labour force of Port Elizabeth had not profited from the industrial expansion of the country, and indeed the city, during the 1940s, but nevertheless trade union activity, much of it led by the Communist Party activists, notably Raymond Mhlaba, was strong. Structural considerations thus interacted with the happenstance of leadership to sharpen the effectiveness of the campaign.

This was a pattern which recurred throughout the 1950s, and indeed in the 1980s. Conflict was spatially unevenly spread. Certain policies impinged more sharply on particular areas. Thus the plans for the destruction of Sophiatown led to a sharp growth in ANC support, and African militancy in general, in Johannesburg. Protests at the rising costs of transport took the form of major bus boycotts in Alexandra, and also in Evaton, part of the burgeoning industrial area on the Vaal river to the south of the Witwatersrand. The opposition to the introduction of Bantu education was concentrated in the townships of the East Rand, such as Brakpan, and in the Eastern Cape, the area with the longest tradition of mission education. On the other hand, the measures to require women to carry passes met with resistance almost across the whole country, largely because they had in principle an impact on at least half the adult African population, if in different ways in the various parts of the country.

Increased Congress militancy led to a swingeing response on the part of the state. The Suppression of Communism Act allowed the government to ban its opponents, by no means necessarily members of the party, from all forms of political activity. By 1955, eleven out of twenty-seven members of the ANC executive were so affected, as were numerous other members of the Congress Alliance. In 1956, furthermore, 156 prominent members of the Alliance were arrested and later charged with treason. For five years, before the trial collapsed, the government attempted to prove that they had conspired to overthrow the state with violence.

Much of the evidence for this conspiracy, which as yet was spurious, derived from the proceedings of the 3,000-strong Congress of the People, held at Kliptown near Johannesburg in April 1955. The suggestion for such a congress came from Z.K. Matthews. A mild-mannered Motswana, Matthews was a long-time congress member and representative of the old African elite who for many years had been a revered professor at the University of Fort Hare. Before it was broken up after two days by police wielding sten guns, the Congress adopted the Freedom Charter, which was to serve as the basis for the ANC programme from then on. Drafted primarily by Lionel Bernstein in a flowing language rare in such political statements, it combines ringing statements of general principle – notably the great slogan 'The People Shall Govern' – with specific proposals deriving above all from the socialist idiom in which Bernstein and many others in the Alliance had come to phrase their political ideals.

This rhetoric did not accord with the experience of many of the Africans involved in nationalist politics. There was also a strong tendency, deriving in its intellectual form from Anton Lembede and A.P. Mda, which stressed the need for psychological liberation. This ran together with a distrust of white involvement in the struggle, whether from liberal missionaries and their adherents or from the largely communist members of the Congress of Democrats. The group of people who propagated this line, and were known as the Africanists (as opposed to the Charterists who were fully committed to the Freedom Charter), were often from the Transvaal or Free State, where the harshness of South Africa's racial relations was more pronounced than in the Cape, or even Natal. Most had come to political maturity after 1948, and thus had no experience of the ultimately repressive liberal consultancy that had preceded the Nationalist victory. Many were teachers, and blocked in their professional advancement by racist legislation. After several years of simmering conflict, in 1958 they broke away from the ANC, to form the Pan-Africanist Congress, electing as their president Robert Sobukwe, a lecturer in African languages at the University of the Witwatersrand in Johannesburg who had first come to prominence by castigating white liberal paternalism at the 1949 graduation address of that liberal paternalist bastion, the University of Fort Hare.

In general, during the 1950s the ANC leadership had paid little attention to the potential for political activism which existed within the

African Reserves of the country. This was in many ways strange. A fair number of the individuals concerned had been brought up in such areas. Against this, the effort required to build a political organisation in South Africa's cities took most of the energy they could spare from earning their livings, and their white communist allies were without direct experience of South Africa's countryside, and only slowly breaking free from the assumption that the revolution would be the work of the proletariat. Internationally, of course, Castro and Guevara were still in the mountains of Cuba, and the lessons of the Chinese revolution, if such they were, still had to be absorbed.

The relative neglect of the Reserves was not for want of issues around which to organise. From the 1930s, and intensifying after World War II, the benign neglect of the Reserves' agricultural economies began to be replaced by an active programme of government intervention. It was believed that the land was overgrazed and the fragile topsoil was washing away into the oceans. This was probably an exaggeration. Although the scars on the land, in terms of *donga*s, were widely evident, the agricultural production of the Reserves remained steady, although of course it declined in per capita terms, and as a proportion of the country's total production. All the same, agricultural officials, in the conviction that they knew best, were demanding a cull of cattle and donkeys and the concentration of the population in villages, with a concomitant redistribution of land among the farmers. Not unnaturally, this heavy-handed involvement in the details of daily life led to considerable peasant resentment.

This coincided with an attempt to restructure the political map of South Africa, with far-reaching consequences for the African Reserves. The idealist visionaries of apartheid realised that total segregation in the cities required the building up of putatively viable economies and political units for their African populations away from the urban centres which would now be for whites only. In addition, they hoped that they could diffuse black South African nationalism by fostering loyalties to the tribal groups from which the Africans were supposed to have come. Thereby, they denied, or tried to reverse, the core process of South African history over the previous half-century at least, namely the social fusion of Africans from all over the country, and from far beyond its borders, in its great cities. They also failed to realise the great fluidity of pre-colonial political units. Rather, they attempted to impose nationalities on unwilling Africans, in the hope that they would emulate the creation and acceptance of Afrikaner nationalism.

In some ways, this entailed a degree of recognition of African participation in the political process of the country. It was symbolised by the renaming of the 'natives' as 'Bantu'. On the other hand, the programme had no regard for the actual aspirations of the mass of the country's black subjects. It was also imposed with great dogmatism. Those who were seen as the legitimate rulers of the African population, the chiefs, became salaried officials of the government, and so were in danger of losing their legitimacy. They had to carry out the orders of the government, or risk dismissal, and the loss of their salaries. But the process of reconstruction in the Reserves allowed those with access to state officials, and the resources of the state in general, to enrich themselves at the expense of their fellow Africans.

Not surprisingly, these developments gave rise to a number of rural uprisings in the late 1950s. Probably the most dramatic was in Pondoland and adjacent areas of the Transkei. There, the increased presence of government agencies was seen as illegitimate, probably as an exercise of the state's occult powers in a much more direct way than previously. The poll tax, for instance, was known as *impundulu*, at once bloodsucker, and the lightning bird by which witches destroy their opponents. Moreover, the state's actions were clearly seen to be driven by malevolence. Stock theft, an endemic evil in all cattle-owning societies, was increasing, and government was not doing anything to prevent it. To the contrary, when vigilante groups, known as *makhulu span*, began to punish those thought to be stock thieves, generally by burning their homesteads, the police and other government officials responded by proceeding against the arsonists, who had some backing in the community, not against the presumed rustlers, who did not. The result was an intensification of the conflict, particularly in the eastern division of Pondoland, where the chief, Botha Sigcau, was unpopular and thought to be illegitimately in office. In 1960, the area effectively went into revolt and a number of Sigcau's councillors were burnt out of the houses. A few were killed. The government's response was to declare a state of emergency, and crush the rebellion, machine-gunning a meeting near Lusikisiki.

Both the government and the ANC claimed that ANC cadres, known to their opponents as 'agitators', were responsible for fomenting the uprising. The evidence for this seems slim. Rather, the ANC leadership, particularly the Transkeian teacher turned journalist Govan Mbeki, tried to claim for the organisation a presence which it did not have, or had only peripherally. In other cases, ANC presence is much clearer, not so much from the national leadership as from individual members of Congress who maintained contact from the urban centres with their own rural regions of origin. This was certainly the case in the two major areas of unrest in the Transvaal, around Zeerust on the border with Botswana and in Sekhukhuneland. In the former case, resistance centred around the decision of the local commissioner to start issuing passes to women. Contacts between the Western Transvaal and migrants from the area resident on the Witwatersrand were particularly close, and even if the ANC did not as such orchestrate the opposition, its inspiration was certainly of importance. On the other hand, those individuals who sided with the government were able to profit from their actions. Lucas Mangope began his rise, which would lead to him becoming president of the Bophuthatswana Bantustan, from his collaboration during the revolt.

In Sekhukhuneland, opposition to the betterment schemes, notably cattle culling, and to the imposition of Bantu authority structures was orchestrated by Sebatakgomo, an organisation of Pedi migrants in Johannesburg, many of whom were members of the ANC. Indeed one of the leaders of the movement, Flag Boshielo, had been banned as a communist. The uprising centred around attacks on those who had taken office under the Bantu authorities scheme, and several of these were assassinated. It would be difficult to say that the ANC leadership actively planned the uprising, but contacts with the law firm which Nelson Mandela had set up with Oliver Tambo in Johannesburg, and with Walter Sisulu, who had been secretary-general of Congress until forced by government to resign in 1954, were close. In the event, though, the rising was put down with considerable force by the government. Twelve men and two women were sentenced to death for their part in the assassinations, although they were ultimately reprieved.

In the course of 1960, the clash between the various African nationalist groups and the government came to a head. Both the ANC and the PAC announced major campaigns against the Pass Laws. In this, they hoped to bring about major reforms in the way the country was governed. In so doing, they were driven largely by their need to compete with each other, and seriously underestimated the power and the ruthlessness of the white-run state.

The PAC had been founded by individuals who lived in the townships of Johannesburg, particularly in Orlando, one of the areas which was incorporated into Soweto – the South Western Townships. Nevertheless, its strength was in those areas where, for one reason or another, the ANC had been unable to establish a presence. These were, above all, the African areas around Cape Town, notably Langa and Nyanga, and in the Vaal townships to the south of Johannesburg, around the newly industrialising towns of Vereeniging and Vanderbijlpark. These latter included Sharpeville, a satellite lying between the two white towns.

The PAC campaign in March of 1960 entailed the marching of large numbers of people to the local police stations, where they would burn their passes. On Monday 21 March, large demonstrations were held throughout the Vaal region. Some 20,000 people converged on the police station at Evaton, and another 4,000 on that of Vanderbijlpark. These demonstrations were dispersed by baton charges and the threat given by low-flying jet aircraft. However, such tactics did not have the same effect for the 5,000 or so people who had gathered in front of Sharpeville police station. Faced with a melee which they could not control, the inexperienced police constables panicked and fired on the crowd, which was armed, at most, with stones. Sixty-nine people, who included eight women and ten children, were killed, and 180 were wounded.

While the shootings at Sharpeville had the effect of dampening down the demonstrations in the Vaal townships, the news of the attacks only exacerbated the activity around Cape Town. These culminated on Wednesday 30 March in a march from Langa and Nyanga into the centre of Cape Town, one of the joint capitals of the country where, at the time, Parliament was sitting. The march was led by Philip Kgosana, famously wearing short trousers. Kgosana, a twenty-three year old from the Western Transvaal, had held a scholarship to the University of Cape Town, but, discouraged by poverty and the difficulty of studying while living in a migrant workers' hostel in Langa, he had dropped out to become a full-time organiser for the PAC. The demonstrations had led to the temporary suspension of the Pass Laws – they were reimposed some ten days later. When the massive crowd arrived at Caledon Square police station in the centre of the city, Kgosana was met by Brigadier

5.4 Some of the dead and wounded outside the Sharpeville police station after the massacre of 21 March 1960.

Terblanche of the police. Terblanche was aware of the temporary military weakness of the state in Cape Town, and had to temporise, afraid that otherwise there would have been a riot which might have gone down as the storming of South Africa's autumn palace. Kgosana, for his part, had reason to fear that the demonstration might end in a blood bath, and in this he was influenced by Patrick Duncan, the son of a former Governor-General who had joined the Liberal Party and was a convinced Gandhian. Kgosana therefore accepted Terblanche's suggestion that he persuade the crowd to disperse and return that evening for an interview with the Minister of Justice.

At this moment, the state snapped out of its indecision. When he returned that evening, Kgosana was arrested, and never got to see the Minister of Justice. A military cordon was thrown round Langa and Nyanga. A state of emergency was proclaimed. On 6 April, both the ANC and the PAC were banned. This was the beginning of a period of repression which, at greater or lesser intensity, was to last for nigh on three decades.

The response of both the ANC and the PAC was to begin to go underground and to start military resistance. They founded military wings, *Umkonto we Sizwe* (the Spear of the Nation, or MK) and *Poqo* (Pure), respectively. They carried out a number of acts of sabotage, and Poqo managed to assassinate a few collaborating chiefs in the Transkei and Ciskei. Quickly, though, both were crippled by government infiltration. Sobukwe and other PAC leaders were arrested, and the rest fled into exile. Mandela and Tambo of the ANC went abroad to gather support. Tambo remained in exile for thirty years, and came to be the ANC's president, holding it together with quiet dignity and great political skill. Mandela returned to the country, and was quickly arrested. Most of the other leaders were captured at a farm in Rivonia, just outside Johannesburg, in July 1963. Two whites among them managed to escape by suborning a warder, but the others among them, including Sisulu and Mbeki, were tried for treason together with Mandela, found guilty and sentenced to prison on Robben Island, where the state confidently expected that they would spend the rest of their lives breaking rocks in the quarry.

From the 1950s until well into the 1970s, South Africa's economy continued to grow very respectably. Between 1948 and 1975, the Gross

Domestic Product increased by an average of about 4.75 per cent per annum. At the same time, the annual growth rate in the country's population was about 3 per cent a year.

At first sight, these figures would seem to indicate a more than satisfactory performance for the economy as a whole, even if the great proportion of the increase was to the benefit of the white minority. In this sense, apartheid could be, and has been, seen as in the interest of the capitalist firms which dominated the country's economy. The most notable of these was Anglo-American, which had diversified out of its initial base in the mining industry until it controlled companies whose value was over half of all those with shares quoted on the Johannesburg Stock Market. By 1987, after buying up the local operations of various foreign firms which had decided to quit the country in response to a call for sanctions and in fear for the future, this proportion had risen to 60 per cent. This made its chairman, Harry Oppenheimer, the most powerful man in the country outside the small coterie around the Prime Minister.

In the short term, such companies benefited from the labour system of apartheid. During the long boom in the world economy, more or less the third quarter of the twentieth century, countries producing primary products, such as South Africa, were in general in an advantageous position. In order to take advantage of these conditions, firms needed a large, cheap and pliable workforce. Apartheid was not a form of forced labour, but the sanctions it imposed on the recalcitrant and the prohibitions it placed on black Trade Union activity weighted matters heavily in favour of the employers. The mining industry, and other employers for whom unskilled labour was crucial, could flourish, and the country's economy as a whole with them.

In the longer term, though, these advantages proved disastrous, and left South Africa singularly ill-equipped to cope with the down-turn in the world economy after about 1973. Until then, there had been no economic imperative to convert the country's low-skilled, low-paid labour force into one whose productivity could rival that of, for instance, those economies of South-East Asia which were industrialising fast. With great foresight, and different political goals, it might have been possible to channel some of the wealth made during the long boom into facilitating such a conversion, at least to some extent. As it was, Bantu education was specifically intended to keep the level of African advancement, and thus of Africans' skills, at a low level. Only from the early 1970s was there an expansion of African education, although the emphasis was probably on quantity rather than quality. The depressed economy after 1970 could not absorb the school-leavers.

As a result, South Africa's manufacturing exports, as good an index as there is of the 'modernisation' of its economy, lagged way below its competitors. Its share of total world trade in manufactured goods declined from 0.78 per cent to 0.27 per cent between 1955 and 1985, and its share in the exports of a group of developing countries, whose starting positions were approximately the same, fell from about an eighth to less than a fiftieth over the same period. Equally, the machine-tool sector totally failed to take part in the growth of the 1950s and 1960s. By 1980, the productivity of the South African labour force was stagnating.

Labour was of course not everything. The state's approach to industrialisation was driven by the ruling group's insecurity, not by a desire to nurture potentially profitable new industries. High tariff walls designed to ensure survival were an excuse for complacency, and South African manufactures slowly became less and less competitive. There were few if any countries outside the Communist bloc in which the state had a greater direct involvement in the economy. The massive projects to produce oil from coal, through SASOL, which eventually produced half the domestic requirements, were clear examples of this, supplementing the state ownership of electricity, iron and steel and railway concerns. The conservatism of state fiscal policies, in part a result of the insecurity which apartheid engendered in the government, meant that the state did not further nurture innovative enterprises. The discouragement and control of the African informal sector prevented the possibility of growth from that quarter which might otherwise have developed through into the rest of the economy. All in all, apartheid had left the country particularly vulnerable to the challenges of the world economy in the last quarter of the century.

After Dr Malan had retired, he had been succeeded by J.G. Strijdom, who was probably dying at the time and certainly was seen as a temporary leader. In 1958, then, Hendrik Verwoerd had come into the office of leader of the National Party and thus Prime Minister. On 9 April 1960, the day after the banning of ANC and PAC, he was shot twice through the head by a white farmer, but, quite remarkably, did not suffer any serious injury. His escape was seen as miraculous, and he himself interpreted it as a sign from God. With this, his control over the National Party, already great, became near enough absolute, and the fanaticism of his rule, already considerable, became confirmed. More generally, the smashing of African opposition, which occurred between Sharpeville and the Rivonia trial, brought about a hardening of apartheid rule, which from then on exhibited its most repressive characteristics.

Under Verwoerd and his successors, the government attempted to pervade all aspects of South African life. In particular, it controlled the media very closely. Three objectives were paramount in this, namely the elimination of statements in opposition to the government, the prevention of infection by liberal and socialist ideas from abroad and the preservation of moral purity. To do this, books, periodicals, music and films were checked, and frequently banned, with the Publications Control Board, set up in 1963, preferring to err on the side of caution, notoriously banning *Black Beauty*, a classic children's story about a girl and her horse, on the basis of its name. The government controlled the radio and refused to allow the establishment of a television service, considering, undoubtedly correctly, that it would not be able to prevent the imported programmes a television service would have had to show from rotting the fabric of South African society.

The sealing off of South Africa from the rest of the world could not be total. Modern pop music could penetrate South Africa from radio stations abroad, particularly in Mozambique. More seriously, the liberal freedoms of the whites could not be extinguished. South Africa was claiming to represent and to uphold the values of Christian Western civilisation. The parliamentary tradition, too, had to be maintained. Elections were held at the prescribed intervals, even if the National Party ensured that it never lost. It could not monopolise parliamentary representation, however. One seat, Houghton in the northern suburbs of Johannesburg, the richest constituency in the country, was held by Helen Suzman for the Progressive Party, which had split off from the United Party. For years, Suzman formed what was in practice a one-woman opposition, as United Party representatives did not fulfill that role with any great vigour. In international terms, she was anything but a leftist. She was, after all, funded by Harry Oppenheimer, the head of the Anglo-American corporation. Her effect was far from negligible, as for instance the prisoners held on Robben Island, whose cause she took up on occasion, have since testified. Equally, churchmen and lawyers, in particular, were able to claim a degree of freedom of action and speech, and, within limits, academics and journalists could continue to expose the injustices of society.

Important though this tradition was, and continues to be, during the high days of apartheid it was at best a minor palliative. From 1960 onwards, with the black opposition crushed and the white opposition emasculated, Verwoerd and the National Party could impose their own vision of society on the country. The principle by which they worked was the denial of any share in a common South African nationality for those who were not whites. Rather, they were thought to belong to one of the following groups: Xhosa, Zulu, Swazi, Tsonga, Ndebele, Venda, North Sotho, South Sotho, Tswana, Indian and Coloured. Each of these groups except for the last two were considered to have their own historic homelands, in which they could develop according to their own traditions – the amaXhosa, by some quirk, had two, the Ciskei and the Transkei. These homelands were generally enormously fragmented, particularly as the consolidation plans which had been put forward in the 1950s were rejected under pressure from the farmers who would have lost their land and in recognition of the primacy of white interests, all apartheid rhetoric notwithstanding. The Transkei was reasonably contiguous, but at the other extreme KwaZulu consisted of eleven separate patches of territory and Bophuthatswana of seven.

Despite this lack of territorial (or for that matter any other form of) integrity, they were all, in the imaginations of apartheid's planners, to be the territories of independent states. Administrations were set up, at considerable cost. Elections were held, but so arranged that even if those in opposition to the government in Pretoria won the votes, they would be outweighed in Parliament by appointed, and thus compliant, chiefs. Eventually, four of the Bantustans did acquire an independence, namely Transkei under Kaiser Matanzima, Ciskei under Lennox Sebe, Bophuthatswana under Lucas Mangope and Venda in the far north. In one sense their independence was farcical, symbolised during the independence ceremony of the Ciskei by the collapse of the pole up which the flag of the new nations was being hoisted. None of them was recognised by any country apart from South Africa and they were all heavily dependent on South Africa for their budget and their internal security, a matter which Pretoria naturally enough took seriously. They might cause minor irritations, as when the Bophuthatswana government set up Sun City, a pleasure resort less than a hundred kilometres from Pretoria where the rich might enjoy those delights – especially gambling and interracial sex – declared illicit by the puritans of the National Party. In general, though, the Bantustan administrations were vicious and corrupt, existing primarily for the enrichment of those who held office within them and as subalterns in the maintenance of order.

Two major consequences derived from the affirmation that every African was to be thought of, not as a South African, but as a citizen of some separate country within its borders. First, as a foreigner, he or she could be deported. People lived under the threat of being removed from where a family might have been living for several generations and dumped in their putative 'homeland' which they might never have visited, where they had little or no opportunity of earning a living and where, at least initially, they had little more than a tent in an insanitary settlement. This was always a possibility even for those with full rights to live in town, and was used as a means of discipline. It was also a continual fact of life for those whose papers were not properly in order, as being 'endorsed out' was added to the fines and imprisonment as punishments under the pass laws.

In addition to these individual banishments, and overshadowing all other nefarious effects of apartheid, was the forced removal of about three and a half million people, over 10 per cent of the country's population, who had the misfortune to be living in the wrong place. The zoning of the country under the Group Areas Act of 1950 between white and black meant that millions of Africans, coloureds and Indians (and very few whites) found that their places of residence had been designated, by officials using small-scale maps and a rigid vision, as land for the occupation of some other racial group, usually the whites. Many of these areas were in effect city suburbs, whose occupants worked in the major cities. Their inhabitants were carted off to the neighbouring Bantustans, from where they had to commute, often two or three hours by bus, to their places of employment, and also had to pay exorbitant rates for the rent of their stands or for water. Others again were driven off land which their forebears had purchased before the passing of the Natives Land Act, or which had been mission stations. In the Tsitsikamma, on the southern coast, there was an area which had been settled by amaMfengu who had chosen the side of the whites in the war of 1835. These inconveniently situated centres of black population were, with a linguistic crassness which rivalled the insensitivity of the policy as a whole, termed 'black spots' and were cleared ruthlessly. Furthermore, as the recession which hit South Africa after 1973 began to bite, and the mechanisation of agriculture became more general, many hundreds of thousands of Africans were forced to leave the farms where they had been working as share-croppers or labour tenants, and they had nowhere to go except to the Bantustans. The result was the creation of great slums, to the extent that the area of Onverwacht, otherwise known as Botshabelo, to the east of Bloemfontein in the Free State grew in population from next to none in 1979 to over half a million seven years later, after it had been proclaimed part of the South Sotho Qwaqwa Bantustan.

The Group Areas Act was also applied to the coloureds and Indians. Although they could not be said to have 'homelands' in South Africa, not even by the Nationalist government, they too were considered to be incipient nations. They acquired parliamentary bodies, which enjoyed little legitimacy among the people who were supposed to elect them, and universities which, like those set up in the various Bantustans, were initially firmly in the grip of conservative Afrikaner academics. The coloureds and Indians were also forced out of the racially mixed districts in which many had been living, particularly in Cape Town. The piecemeal eviction of coloureds from Cape Town's suburbs caused much individual suffering, as families were driven to desolate new townships on the sands of the Cape flats, notably Mitchells Plain. The homes they had vacated were often bought up cheaply by speculators close to the National Party top and sold on, perhaps after renovation, at a great profit.

The one place where this form of profiteering did not prove possible was the area known as District Six, an old, rough, working-class quarter close to the centre of Cape Town. Though romanticised in retrospect, it was nevertheless the heart of coloured culture in the city, much as Sophiatown had been for the African bourgeoisie of Johannesburg. It contained, for instance, the main coloured secondary schools, of high quality and with many Trotskyite intellectuals among the staff. In the course of the 1960s, it was declared a slum and a white area, its inhabitants evicted and its buildings, except for the churches and mosques, razed. Potentially, it was then some of the most valuable real estate in the country, but for once the government was unable to persuade developers or firms to take on projects in the symbolically polluted ground, and the area remains a tract of wasteland.

A second effect of the Bantustan policy was intended to be the nurturing of national consciousness among the various groups the government had identified. With one exception, these ideas were not accepted, although, particularly in parts of the Transvaal and the Free State, descent could be, and was, used as one of the weapons in the struggle for the limited resources of the Bantustans.

The exception was among the amaZulu. There were two aspects to this. In the first place, through the first half of the twentieth century, strenuous efforts were made by a variety of groups to resuscitate ideas of Zulu nationhood and to extend them to people whose forebears had never been the subjects of Shaka and his successors. At the core of this process was a revival in the fortunes and influence of the Zulu royal family. Sponsored by *amakholwa* intellectuals hoping to anchor their own political position through this alliance, and by the sugar barons of northern Natal who saw in Zulu 'traditionalism' a welcome counterweight to, for instance, the radicalism of the ICU, King Solomon kaDinizulu, whose reign began in 1913, was able to claim from the officials of the South African state respect and power for the monarchy at least the equal of any other black ruler in the country. This power meant that potential followers were prepared to identify with the royal house. In the rural areas of northern Natal, in particular, the monarchy and its representatives came to guarantee the status of the migrant labourers as heads of their own households, and thus confirm their adult masculinity. In return, these men would accept the tenets of Zulu traditionalism, an ideology and a way of life recreated each generation, as all ideologies which survive must be.

Secondly, these ideas were used with great subtlety and political finesse in interaction with the Bantustan policy of the South African government from the late 1960s onwards. At the centre of this was Chief Mangosotho Gatsha Buthelezi. A high Zulu aristocrat, he could claim to be the hereditary prime minister of the Kingdom – though whether such an office had existed was disputed. He had been at the University of Fort Hare in the late 1940s and had joined the ANC Youth League, but his political, and above all his economic and social, ideas always had more in common with the conservative ANC elite that the Youth League had displaced. All the same, he had connections with almost all the old ANC top. At least in their early days, his actions within the KwaZulu bantustan had the private support of the ANC leaders in exile. The idea that apartheid might be opposed from within the institutions it had created was attractive at a time when almost all other forms of opposition had been crushed, and Buthelezi never exceeded certain boundaries, never accepting independence for KwaZulu, for instance.

Once in power in the KwaZulu Bantustan, however, Buthelezi was able to use the benefits of office in order both to intensify Zulu nationhood, by accentuating the symbols out of its past, and to entrench his own position. This latter he did by turning the Bantustan government into a political machine, so that adherence to Inkatha, which had begun as a movement for cultural renewal and became a political party under his leadership, was both represented as an inherent part of Zulu identity and recognised to be essential for any form of economic success – including drawing a state pension – and even for physical survival.

From the late 1950s, and particularly after Sharpeville, South Africa's policies were becoming increasingly anomalous in comparison with what was occurring elsewhere in the continent, and in the world. Initially, this did not greatly concern the National Party leadership. Indeed, the condemnation which the country received only strengthened them in their desire to turn South Africa into a Republic. This was done following a referendum in 1961, the first election in which the National Party received a majority of the white vote. In the same wave of Afrikaner and South African nationalism, formal ties with the British Empire were broken as the country left the Commonwealth in the same year.

In 1966, Hendrik Verwoerd was stabbed to death on the floor of Parliament by a messenger, apparently without clear political motive. This event stunned the Nationalists and, according to legend, was greeted by the coloured taxi-drivers of Cape Town driving round the city with their horns blaring in celebration. He was succeeded by Balthazar Johannes Vorster, often, and surprisingly, anglicised to John, who was relatively junior within the cabinet and unforgiven by its elder members for his participation in the *Ossewabrandwag*, in the course of which he had spent some years in gaol during the war for nazi sympathies. As

Minister of Police, though, he had built up a reputation for toughness which probably ensured his victory in the party's internal elections. His was to be a rule which relied heavily on newly established secret police forces, notably the acronymically appropriate Bureau of State Security under his fellow World War II prisoner, Hendrik van den Bergh.

At home, Vorster's government continued and intensified the repression of its predecessor. Its greatest challenge, though, came beyond the formal borders of what was now the Republic. In 1965, the High Commission Territories became independent as Botswana, Lesotho and Swaziland. In the latter two cases, this was not a problem for the South African government, as the two Kingdoms were not able, or prepared, to aid any threats to the Republic. Botswana was another matter. Its first President was Sir Seretse Khama, who in 1952 had been deposed as Chief of the Bamangwato tribe for marrying a white woman, largely because the British were wary of apartheid South Africa's reaction. A combination of enlightened government and a mineral bonanza allowed the country to assert a genuine independence.

South Africa's relations with the countries further to the north were more problematic. The achievement of independence by the great majority of African colonies had cut the Republic off from what had always been its natural hinterland, and, as its policies became increasingly anomalous in the new world of the 1960s, turned it into a pariah, albeit, in African terms, an immensely rich and powerful one. It was, however, bordered by three other such pariahs, Rhodesia, whose tiny white minority had resisted the trend towards African majority rule and, under Ian Smith, unilaterally declared the country independent in 1965, and the two Portuguese colonies of Angola and Mozambique, whose colonial rulers still believed that grandeur depended on overseas possessions. Faced with guerrilla wars in both colonies, and also in Guinea-Bissau in West Africa, the Portuguese government finally crumbled, and in 1975 the insurgents took over the two countries.

Whether or not their diagnosis was accurate, the South African rulers saw these events as a potential threat to their own survival. For as long as possible, they bolstered the Smith government, from their point of view not unreasonably as the first guerrilla attacks were made with the help of units from the ANC in exile. They attempted to neutralise the former Portuguese colonies by abetting movements of armed opposition, RENAMO against the FRELIMO government in Mozambique and UNITA against the MPLA leaders of Angola. The result was massive destruction, from which the two countries have yet to recover. Against this, from 1975, the South African army began to be deployed not just in Rhodesia but also in Angola, where it severely overestimated its own capacities and suffered a major defeat.

The crushing of the ANC and the PAC entailed, temporarily, an end to organised political resistance. Naturally enough, it did not lead to the acceptance by the mass of blacks of the institutions of apartheid. The difficulty was to find a forum within which individual dissatisfaction could be collected to form a collective challenge to the state.

Such collectivities emerged in two locations within South African society. The first derived from the increasing number of Black South Africans who were attending the country's universities. They coalesced around the charismatic figure of Steve Biko, a man from the Eastern Cape who was studying medicine in Natal. Biko found his allies in those like him who were rejecting the dominant role whites played even in the National Union of South African Students, at that stage probably the most radical legal body in the country. Significantly, Biko's first main platform was in the apparently innocuous Universities Christian Movement. From there, he organised the South African Students Organisation, which soon found its roots on the black campuses of the country, and within a couple of years was spreading downwards into the schools and upwards to create the Black Peoples Convention, an umbrella institution which was to act as a political party.

The Black Consciousness movement, as the organisations under Biko's inspiration came to be known, had two prime concerns. The first, as befitted a political stream which had its origins, in part at least, in a Christian movement, was a great stress on individuals' responsibility for liberation, almost as salvation. The rejection of white organisations was not a rejection of the place of whites within the country, indeed within the fight against apartheid; rather it came from a recognition of the positive necessity for Africans (and for that matter coloureds and Indians) to take, and not to wait to be given. The second was an appreciation that the failure of in particular the PAC around 1960 had been a consequence of impatience, and that, in consequence, it was important not to be too hasty in seeking confrontations with the government.

With their roots in the South African universities, the founders of the

Black Consciousness movement had little immediate affinity with the working class of the cities, who were underpaid, largely unskilled and, as the depression of the 1970s began to bite, increasingly insecure in their jobs. After a decade of slowly rising African real wages, a sharp upswing of the rate of inflation began seriously to affect the standard of living of African workers. They formed the second location for resistance in the early 1970s. Beginning in Durban in 1973, a series of strikes broke out. In the first three months of that year, over 60,000 workers came out. As Africans in South Africa began to take heart from the collapse of the Portuguese empire, and the victory this represented for the insurgents, these strikes signalled the end of the hiatus of political calm which through the 1960s had seemed like the victory of apartheid.

Industrial unrest was paralleled by unrest in the schools. The Verwoerdian logic had been to restrict secondary education for blacks in the towns, in the assumption that the Bantustan systems would perform the required task. Against this, the age cohort of Africans of school going age was increasing rapidly. The Bantustan schools were overloaded anyway. Urban youngsters did not wish, and could not afford, to board away in the countryside. Schools in the towns were having to take on more and more pupils, but their funding was far behind what was necessary. Employers were suffering from the underdevelopment of their labour force. African education was an epitome of the contradictions at the heart of apartheid, made worse by Vorster's decision to appoint Dr Andries Treurnicht, chairman of the Broederbond and the most fervent of believers in Verwoerd's gospel, as Under-Minister for Bantu Education. Treurnicht decreed that certain subjects, notably mathematics, be taught in Afrikaans, both lowering the quality of education – there were too few teachers who could teach maths anyway, let alone in Afrikaans – and demonstrating state power. An appointment meant as a sop to the National Party's right wing became the trigger for a student revolt.

In the winter of 1976, pupils at a number of schools in Soweto began to demonstrate, under the leadership of the South African Students' Movement, the Black Consciousness organisation working in secondary education. On 16 June, a group of about 15,000 youths were met by the police, who first tried to disperse them with tear gas and then fired on them, killing two. The photograph of Hector Petersen, aged twelve, being carried through Soweto mortally wounded shocked the world and became one of the icons of apartheid's brutality. In Soweto itself, youths went on the rampage, killing two whites unfortunate enough to be caught unprotected on its wild streets, and burning many shebeens,* as the youths saw alcohol as degrading, wrecking families and holding the adults in thrall. Within days, the revolt had spread to the other townships on the Witwatersrand, to Cape Town, where the coloureds, under the influence of Black Consciousness, made common cause with the Africans, and to the Eastern Cape.

In the weeks that followed, the uprising was put down with great harshness. Hundreds of blacks were arrested and many were killed. Biko himself remained at large for more than a year, but when finally caught he was beaten up, slung in the back of a truck and driven from the Eastern Cape to Johannesburg. He did not survive the journey. Many others were sent to gaol, or fled the country. In both cases, they came into contact with the ANC, which had not predicted the revolt but profited from it, gaining both recruits for MK and activists who were to continue their political work once their sentences had ended. It was to prove the resuscitation of the organisation.

The government's initial reaction to the uprising was repression. In the years that followed, however, it began cautiously to move away from the dogmas of Verwoerdian apartheid. In two senses, then, the Soweto revolt was the beginning of the end of apartheid rule.

---

* Unlicensed, and thus illegal, drinking houses known throughout Southern Africa by the name Irish policemen in Cape Town had given them at the beginning of the century.

6

The costs of apartheid

Throughout the twentieth century, the population of South Africa has been growing. Between Union and 1996, the total number of South Africans increased sixfold, from just under 6 million to just under 38 million. Until 1948, the proportion of whites in the population remained more or less constant, at around 21 per cent, but then began to decline sharply, until by 1988 it was only around 14 per cent. (In 1996 the census did not concern itself with such classifications.) The proportion of coloureds and Indians remained fairly steady, except during the 1950s, which saw a rise of over one per cent in the coloureds' share, presumably as a result of stricter classification following the Population Registration Act, not of major demographic shifts.

The conclusion that can be drawn from these figures is of course that the Black population has continued to grow steadily and sharply. Between 1910 and 1948 it grew at, on average, 1.92 per cent per annum, and in the first thirty-one years of National Party rule at 3.14 per cent per annum. From the 1980s, and perhaps earlier, this rate of growth declined, until by the 1990s it was below 2 per cent.

At the macro level, the reasons for this population growth are quite clear. There have been no major famines or other crises of subsistence in the country since the Rinderpest epizootic of the 1890s. The only major population crash was caused by the influenza pandemic of 1919. A steadily high birth rate means that the black population has continued to increase. It is only recently that the birth rate has begun to fall, as increasingly the costs of bringing up children have come to exceed the benefits which could be gained from their labour. This was not realised sufficiently by the demographers, so that after 1970 the country's population was consistently overestimated, eventually by 10 per cent, or four million people.

In general, harvest failures caused by drought or other reasons have led to hardship, but the transport of food from other parts of the country, or on occasion from overseas, has meant that deaths from starvation, or from malnutrition-induced disease, have become chronic, not acute and all-compassing. The ending of the periodic massive crises of subsistence – famines, in other words – and to a lesser extent of the annually recurring hungry months before the harvest which had controlled the country's population in pre-colonial times did not of course necessarily lead to an improvement in the general standard of life and health of the mass of the black population in normal times. Rather the characteristics of poverty changed. It was no longer universal and catastrophic. Rather it became selective and chronic. Individuals with access to resources, either through the labour market or because of political privilege, have prospered, at least temporarily. For the rest, the increase in population has meant that the mere ability to labour has not in any way been a guarantee of sufficient subsistence. The policies of apartheid only served to accentuate this division.

The course of impoverishment can be seen most clearly in the rural labour reserves, which may indeed be said to have included Lesotho. One, at least some of them had reasonably prosperous economies. Both Lesotho and Pondoland in the Transkei, for instance, exported grain to the urban centres of South Africa in the later nineteenth century. Furthermore, as was pointed out in Chapter 4, wages from mine labour were invested into the agricultural economy, so that the cattle herd of Pondoland, for instance, reached its peak in the 1920s. However, in the long term this quite literally eroded the basis for agricultural production. First, the cattle and sheep began to eat away those areas where a variety of wild spinaches grew, which had provided important vitamins for women and children. Then, as the general level of grazing deteriorated, and sheep began to consume more and more of it, far too little milk was available, particularly in dry winters, for those children who had just been weaned. Infant mortality was high, and those who survived were often stunted. Slowly, too, the agricultural side of the reserve economy began to crumble. What were said to be rural, agricultural districts became ever more dependent on the import of food, usually at

6.1 S.E.K. Mqhayi, here photographed in 1926, was renowned as
the finest Xhosa *imbongi* of his generation. In the past every
young man would try his hand at producing and singing
izibongo, or praise poems, for himself, or of his cattle. These
would always be highly metaphorical and allusive. The most
talented might be chosen to perform in praise of the chief, and
would thus acquire considerable status. The translation 'praise
poem', however, though standardly used, is not accurate, since
the genre allowed for the not so veiled criticism of the individual
so praised. The genre was maintained, not merely in the
countryside, but also within urban political settings. Not merely
did ANC meetings, for instance, often include the praises of the
leader, Albert Luthuli during his presidency, but Trade Union
gatherings would increasingly be harangued by an *imbongi*
intoning the praises of the Union. At his inauguration as

prices inflated for the profit of European traders, from the subsidised European-owned maize farms of the High Veld. By the mid-1950s, Transkei farming families produced on average nearly half of what they consumed; by the end of the 1970s this had fallen to under a sixth.

The steady collapse of the Reserves' agricultural economies turned many once lush areas, for instance in the Ciskei, in Zululand, in Sekhukhuneland or in Lesotho, into treeless near-deserts. In 1980, the rural population density in the Reserves ran from 29 to the square kilometre in Bophuthatswana (which included large tracts of what were semi-deserts even before the coming of colonial rule) through 55 in the Transkei, 65 in Lebowa, 82 in the Ciskei to a staggering 193 in Kwandebele and 298 in the mountainous enclave of Qwa Qwa. For comparison, the average population density of the non-reserve areas of the Cape Province was two to the square kilometre, and that of the Transvaal eleven. Places like Kwandebele and Qwa Qwa had ceased to be farming areas in any reasonable sense of the word.

6.1 (*cont*).
president, Nelson Mandela too received the praises – in this instance uncritical – of an *imbongi*.

In Lesotho, at least, the genre was also transformed to provide an opportunity for social commentary, and was no longer tied to individuals. Men used this sung poetry, or *lifela*, to bemoan the dangers and the barbarism of the Republic, to whose mines they went as migrant labourers. Crossing the Caledon river, they entered the land of the cannibals, or of the wild Bushmen, those two potent symbols for those who were outside the ordered, civilised world of the village community and the Mountain Kingdom. In the *lifela*, the migrants described their longing for the rural life, the trains which took them to the mines and the snares of town women among whom they might move. Some women, on the other hand, began to take up what had been an exclusively male genre. They sang in the shebeens of Lesotho (and no doubt on the Witwatersrand as well), as part of the entertainment. Their message, though, was not of that submissive femininity which the men expected, but rather of the aggressive, individualistic entrepreneurship necessary to survive and prosper in the world they had entered.

Other women continued to practise the other main form of oral art, the Ntsomi folk-tales, which contained a considerable proportion of the country's lore.

6.2 This photograph, taken in KwaZulu in the 1980s, shows the
ecological degredation, including a great *donga* running through
the centre of the picture, of many of the Reserves.

In all the Reserves, communal grazing areas, with only distrusted
chiefs to control access, deteriorated rapidly. Erosion, everywhere a
danger in a country where grass cover can be thin as the torrential rains
of early summer arrive, stripped much of the country of its topsoil. A
simple path could quickly become the bed of a rivulet, and within a few
years a deep *donga*, a scar through the earth many feet deep. Erosion
was not irreversible. In the 1930s the wheat fields of the Swartland to
the north of Cape Town had been a terrible warning to the rest of the
country; they have largely recovered. However, to do this required concerted action and its acceptance by all those who managed the land.
This latter could probably never have been achieved in the conditions of
South Africa's Reserves, where overcrowding was exacerbated by the
regular dumping of those the apartheid government thought unwanted
in the cities. It certainly could not happen through the 'betterment'
schemes which that government's authoritarianism imposed on what
were euphemistically still known as rural areas.

The principles of betterment entailed the concentration of the population into villages, where schools and health centres could be more
efficiently served, and where the surplus population could be held. The

land was then to be divided amongst the farming population in economic units. In the event, the plots that were handed out were rarely of economic size, and with virtually no sources of employment in the new villages, they quickly became slums. In general, though, they were not as bad as places like Botshabelo in the eastern Free State or the Winterveld and Kwandebele to the north of Pretoria, where the only employment was a three-hour bus journey away in the country's capital.

Given the hopelessness of life in the Reserves, increasing numbers of men and, particularly, women came to settle illegally in the cities of South Africa. There of course they were subject to influx control regulations and ran a continual risk of being 'endorsed out', back to the Reserves, by court order. At the peak, in 1975, the single magistrate's court of Langa, a black township of Cape Town, was convicting over a hundred pass offenders *a day*, and it was not the only such court in the city, let alone the country. Nevertheless, the pressure was inexorable. Those who could do so took residence with relatives, no doubt often straining the bonds of kinship. Others built shacks in the back yards of householders with residential rights, through their rent increasing the benefits provided by the essentially arbitrary decision of the state to grant such rights. Others again set up informal settlements, or 'squatter camps' as they were known in the jargon of apartheid.

The best known of these settlements was Crossroads, in the sandy Cape Flats just to the east of Cape Town. Through a quirk of the South African judicial system, it received the status of emergency camp in early 1976, and thus escaped the wholesale clearance of such areas in the wake of the Soweto uprising. It thus grew quickly, and by the mid-1980s it and the areas around it had a population of well over 100,000. Lying as it did almost under the flight path of Cape Town's airport, what happened there was particularly visible to whites from the city's liberal establishment, and indeed to overseas journalists. It was from the beginning a test of the Government's resolve to regulate the urbanisation of Africans, particularly as the Western Cape had long been declared an area where coloureds should be granted all possible preference (over Africans, not over whites) in the labour market. It was also a place where people found new ways to survive in difficult circumstances, and in the process evolved political structures with which to do so.

At the heart of Crossroads politics was Johnson Ngxobongwana. In the course of the 1980s he worked his way up to become the archetypi-

6.3 Tin shacks in the 'squatter camp' of Crossroads in the
1980s.

cal local warlord of the South African townships. With an initial political and, probably, financial capital acquired as chairman of a ward
committee within the settlement, and later expanded through the unofficial sponsorship of the state, he gathered a substantial following of
toughs. These, known as the *witdoeke* from the cloth they wore round
their heads to identify themselves in a fight, he used to eliminate rival
leaders, to sideline women's groups who in the early years of Crossroads
had been influential political actors and to confront the radical youth
groups which emerged as national political struggles evolved after 1984.
Finally, in 1986, the *witdoeke* drove through the satellite camps around
Crossroads, over which Ngxobongwana had yet to establish his power,
burning the houses which had been built and expelling an estimated
70,000 people. This was done with the complicity of the South African
government.

The rise of Ngxobongwana was a particularly flagrant example of a
phenomenon which was repeated widely, particularly in the 1980s.
Throughout South Africa, strong men were able to assert their control
over stretches of territory. By no means all of them were under the spon-

sorship of the apartheid state, or chose its side in the conflicts of the 1980s and 1990s. All, however, took advantage of the absence of elementary institutions of civil power on the ground, notably the police force. The police were too heavily used as a paramilitary force to crush resistance for them to be able to maintain law and order as the mass of the population would have hoped. Only about 6 per cent of the country's police were actually engaged in attempting to solve crimes, and they were disproportionately concerned with those crimes committed against whites. The opportunities for offering protection at a price, for instance so that wage-earners had a reasonable chance of reaching their homes alive and with their wage packets still in their pockets, were great. These services could only too easily turn into protection rackets, imposed by force, and into the establishment of tightly controlled political fiefdoms.

The violence of South African society was immense. In the mid-1980s, over a quarter of all black deaths in Cape Town, Johannesburg and Pietermaritzburg, at least, were not natural, and over half of these were the result of homicide. The rest were the consequence of accidents, on the roads (the majority), at work or at home. This violence long preceded the political violence of the mid-1980s, which in any event made up only a small proportion of the deaths by direct human agency. It can be attributed to at least three major sets of causes. First, the violence of colonial conquest and that required to maintain the racial order continually made itself felt at all levels of society. The government waged war both beyond the boundaries of the Republic and within the country itself, smashing communities by force. It killed and maimed those it perceived to be its opponents, sometimes through random terror, sometimes brutally in police cells, sometimes by judicial execution. To aid in this repression, it had no difficulty in recruiting black (and for that matter white) henchmen.

Secondly, the social degradation of life in the townships and dumping grounds of the Reserves fed the violence. People with no other hopes for advancement were led to prey on their fellows. Certainly from the 1940s on, successful gangsters could provide romantic role-models. Many followed the hope of the *totsis* of Sophiatown in Johannesburg to 'live well, die young and leave a good-looking corpse'. And the criminal lifestyle became only more attractive with the removal to the faceless townships. In the Cape Town of the 1940s, District Six was ruled by its gangs.

There were streets where the police, not yet a paramilitary force, did not dare go. In the townships of the Cape Flats, their sway only increased. Throughout the country, too, the hopelessness of life led to rampant alcoholism and drug-usage, particularly *dagga* (marijuana) and mandrax, a South African preparation from Indian medicines. Both fed the need for money and removed such scruples as may have existed. Then, the arming of white suburbia, for protection against attacks, led to the ready presence of firearms taken in those attacks that were successful.

Thirdly, the violence of South African society clearly derives in part from the ways in which young men, in particular, were brought up, by their peers, by their parents and by society at large. It was generally accepted within African societies, and indeed by wide sections of white society, that young men should be competitive, aggressive and brave. These were values which were inculcated to white men, for instance during their time of service in the South African Defence Force, and in pre-colonial times to Africans, when they functioned to develop an effective fighting force. The time spent as warriors had been an integral part of the life-cycle, between the initiation of a group of young men into an age regiment and their marriages, and even afterwards they might be called up as necessary. The socialising processes sustaining such personalities and such ideas of how a young man should behave were only modified slowly in the course of the twentieth century, and faster for the better educated and more middle-class than for the mass of South Africans.

In the past the potential danger of such groups was held in check by the dominance of the fully adult men, for instance through their control of the cattle a youth had to acquire before he could begin to pay bride-wealth and thus marry. However, through the twentieth century structures of authority within the family broke down. In the rural areas, men were generally away, serving terms of migrant labour, and thus could not physically impose the deference their position entailed. There were areas where 90 per cent of first births were to unmarried mothers. Even when the men were present, they rarely possessed the resources without which their supremacy was empty and soon challenged. In the towns, too, their social impotence was all too evident, and frequently gave way to despair and drunkenness. Social institutions within African society could no longer control its young men, and these were at best sporadically replaced by others, for instance in the schools. Education was

6.4 *Tsotsi*s in Johannesburg in the 1950s. In the 1940s and 1950s, the gangsters of Johannesburg, particularly Sophiatown, and also of Cape Town, and no doubt of other cities, were often inspired in their style of dress and so forth by the B-movies coming out of Hollywood. Hence the broad hats and flash American car. Known as *tsotsi*s, they formed some of the most visible, and most feared, of black Johannesburg's inhabitants. For this reason, the argot developed in the towns became known as *tsotsitaal*, the language of the *tsotsi*s. It is a constantly evolving creole, with an Afrikaans syntactic base but a lexicon which derives in very large measure from Bantu languages, particularly isiZulu.

rarely seen as a route to social betterment. As a result, the pressures towards, and the attractions of, a criminal way of life were not sufficiently counteracted.

Certainly during the 1980s, moreover, the boundaries between criminality and political action became blurred. During the course of the township revolt, which will be discussed in more detail in the next chapter, young men grasped the opportunity to impose themselves on their surroundings. The destruction of beer halls and shebeens was a way of controlling such income as did come into the family, and of counteracting some of the worst symptoms of degradation. The conflicts within many African communities were seen as being between the young, known as the 'Comrades', and the 'Fathers'. The latter were often seen as working to bolster apartheid, but this was rarely their explicit aim. Many would have been shocked at the idea. Rather they hoped to re-establish what they saw as the proper relationship between the generations, a relationship which had been destroyed by the dehumanisation of township life, and thus indirectly by apartheid.

With the demise of subsistence peasantry, survival and welfare came to depend on access to a cash income. Even in parts of the Reserves, those with access to land might well decide that it made sense to grow high-grade maize for sale and purchase their foodstuffs from the local traders. They might also grow *dagga*, at least when they had some hope that their crop could escape the attentions of government anti-narcotics agents. Elsewhere, the tiny plots that were available could be used to grow small quantities of sorghum and vegetables to supplement what was bought, not as the basis for subsistence. And in the towns, even these options were rarely, if ever, available.

Given these circumstances, the distribution of income was of crucial importance. It was of course highly unequal. In the early 1970s, the richest 20 per cent of the South African population owned 75 per cent of the country's wealth (compared for instance to just under 40 per cent in the United States). At the end of the decade, the standard measure of income inequality, the Gini coefficient, was the highest for any of the fifty-seven states in the world for which information was available. Income was, not surprisingly, closely correlated with racial status. In 1983, the disposable income per capita of Asians was 37 per cent of that of whites, of coloureds 26 per cent, of Africans in the towns 22 per cent and of Africans outside the towns incredibly just over 6 per cent. Measured in terms of the cost of living, for which a minimum living level was calculated, nearly two-thirds of all Africans, and over four-fifths of those Africans living in the Reserves, were in dire poverty. There were some indications that the proportion of Africans so afflicted was declining. During the 1970s the amount of the country's wealth held by the richest 20 per cent declined to 61 per cent. What this meant, though, was that the level of inequality within the African population was increasing, while the gross differences between Africans and whites were declining somewhat. However, given the level of population growth, the total number of Africans living below the level of reasonable subsistence was actually increasing.

Poverty had numerous consequences for the basic physical health of the South African people. Certain specific diseases, including sexually transmitted diseases (syphilis, gonorrhoea and, latterly, AIDS) have spread very widely in the country as a result of its integration as a single social network. Probably the most important such sickness, historically, has been tuberculosis. Before the later nineteenth century, the disease had existed at a low level, if at all, in the country. Thereafter, through the first half of the twentieth century, the incidence of the disease among Africans grew alarmingly. The mining compounds and the slum-yards of the major cities provided almost ideal conditions for infection. Moreover, sick workers on the mines were initially sent back to the countryside as soon as they were diagnosed, thus allowing them to spread the disease throughout the country and beyond its borders. The same process was at work during the 1960s and 1970s, though not as a result of conscious decisions. Rather the recurrent forced relocations of Africans from the cities hit those most likely to be in bad health, and thus susceptible to TB. It also removed them from the centres of medical care. Thus, while there was a steady decline in the number of cases reported, and also a much better chance of curing sufferers as the pharmaceutical industry world-wide at least temporarily was able to provide effective drugs against TB, the actual decline among Africans was almost certainly far less than was claimed.

In this, the incidence of TB provides a model for a wide variety of medical matters. There can be no doubt that on average the whole South African population benefited from medical advances, and probably also from an increase in the standard of living, and thus of health. This is clear, for instance, with regard to one of the most sensitive indices of general well-being, namely infant mortality. Thus, between 1960 and 1985 the proportion of children dying before their first birthday declined from 135 per thousand to 78. Since Africans were by far the largest group in the population, and even in 1960 had by far the highest rate, this decline of over 40 per cent must have entailed a substantial improvement of average African health. Averages, however, can be famously misleading, since they reduce a range of variation to a single value. In this case, the range could be very great indeed. For instance, from a high point of around 280 per thousand in 1950, the African infant mortality rate in Cape Town decreased to only around a seventh of that by the mid-1980s, though it was still three times the white rate. A similar decline was evident for Soweto, for instance, and for most official townships at least until the late 1980s. There are qualifications. This figure undoubtedly did not include all of those dying in infancy in the informal settlements such as Crossroads. All the same the contrast with rural black South Africans was enormous. Among them, infant mortality was running at or over 100 per thousand. Once again, there were clear advantages in being one of the relatively privileged under apartheid's ever finer dissection of the population. Those who were living legally in the Cape Town townships, or in Soweto, were likely to be employed and reasonably housed and have access to health services. The others were cast out into desperation.

The divisions generated by apartheid only became stronger during the 1970s and 1980s as unemployment increased sharply. In the long depression of the last quarter of the twentieth century, the formal labour market could not absorb those hundreds of thousands of young men and women who every year were seeking jobs for the first time. In particular, the demand for unskilled manual labour, the mainstay of the old apartheid economy, stagnated. Except for short-lived peaks around 1976 and again a decade later, gold mining employment remained more or less static. The mechanisation of agriculture entailed a slow decline in the number of full-time workers, for instance in the maize country of the Western Transvaal, and a precipitous drop in the numbers of men, women and children employed for seasonal labour at harvest time. In the six magisterial districts of the area, the requirement for such workers dropped from 105,000 in 1968 to just over 40,000 in 1981.

The vagaries of registration make it difficult to give accurate figures for South African unemployment. Nevertheless, the information that is available shows a sharp rise in unemployment during the 1970s, to around 20 per cent of the economically active population by 1980. Thereafter, matters became worse. Through the 1980s, there was an actual decline in the absolute number (let alone the proportion) of people employed in the formal economy. By the early 1990s, the National Manpower Commission estimated that 4.9 million people, or

39 per cent of those who might have wished for a job, could not find one within the formal economy, a figure which was probably fairly accurate, since the overestimation of the population was greatest for those who were still children. This unemployment hit young blacks particularly hard. The same commission estimated that, in 1960, 70 per cent of entrants to the labour market were able to find a job. By the 1980s this figure had fallen to 14 per cent, and by 1992 the estimate was that only one potential new worker in twenty would actually find a job.

These figures refer only to those within the formal economy, that is to say those who have a job with the state, with a registered company, on a white-owned farm or officially in domestic service. Fully half of those who are formally unemployed have some source of income from economic activities outside these sectors. This had of course long been a feature of South African towns. In nineteenth-century Port Elizabeth, the men who carried goods and people through the surf worked for their own account and uncontrolled, as did the guilds of Zulu washer-men who did Durban's laundry. Early Johannesburg gave plentiful opportunities for the proliferation of many economic activities, servic-ing both the white and the black communities. Indeed, at this stage, it is doubtful whether a meaningful distinction could be drawn between formal and informal employment, at least when, for instance, mine labour is discounted.

Some of the activities within the informal sector were for a long time tolerated by the white authorities, particularly when they either served the whites or, as for instance with the various forms of African healing, did not significantly compete with them. Others led to chronic conflict. The most notable such area was with regard to the brewing and sale of beer, and of alcoholic beverages in general. This had proved to be a major source of income for African women coming to town, whether as a supplement to the wages of their husbands or as a means for allowing them independence from any man. Some brewed barrels irregularly; others progressed to keeping shebeens. These might serve European liquor as well as the sorghum-based *utshwala*, even instead of it if they were aiming at a high-status clientele. They might also provide other forms of recreation, notably sex and music. It was from the shebeens of Johannesburg that South African popular music began its development.

The assault on African liquor production and sales was continuous. In the mid-1950s there were over 200,000 convictions annually under the

6.5 A beer hall in Johannesburg in the 1950s. Much of South
Africa's history can be written through its drinking habits and
regulations. In the Western Cape after emancipation, farmers
encouraged their labourers' addiction to alcohol, making them a
pliant if inefficient workforce. Respectable Christian – and for
that matter Muslim – society always advocated and practised
temperance. For urbanising Africans, there were two possible
places to drink, the beer hall and the shebeen. The former was
legal, and usually owned by the municipalities, which derived a
large proportion of the income they needed to run the townships
from the sale of *utshwala*. However, the mass-produced beer, the
limitation on choice and the sterile, unwelcoming ambience were
widely rejected. The alternative was the shebeen. These have
been of many types. Some have been quiet domestic parlours;
others seen as seats of iniquity, selling *dagga*, sex and illegally
distilled spirits, often full of impurities and sometimes lethal.
Most were somewhere in between. The higher class of shebeen
sold beer, wine and brandy of European style, although
produced in South Africa, and perhaps some imported whisky;
others concentrated on *utshwala*, usually brewed on the
premises. In general they were run by women, known as shebeen
queens, and brewing activities provided important income
opportunities for women in the cities. Always, though, drinking
establishments were seats of conflict, under threat at various
times from women who hoped to deflect their menfolk's income
away from the beerhall to the home or to the home brewery,
from the local authorities, who long saw shebeens as a threat
both to their own monopoly and to law and order, and in the

liquor laws. Raids on shebeens and on township brewers were a regular occurrence, and formed part of the expenses of the shebeen queens, as these publicans were known. In twelve months in 1935–6, for instance, over 11,000 gallons of liquor were drained down the streams of the East Rand town of Springs alone. In part, the reason for this was financial. In 1908, the Natal legislature allowed municipalities to establish monopolies over the sale of *utshwala*. The idea was that African men should be limited in their drinking to large beerhalls, where they were under some degree of surveillance and where the profits would accrue to the town council. In this way, they could finance the costs of African locations without them being any charge on European ratepayers. It was a system which spread throughout the Union after 1910, and indeed further, for instance into Southern Rhodesia. Since the municipality paid the location superintendents and the police, the pressure to maintain a campaign against interlopers on municipal monopolies was continuous, if fluctuating in intensity.

There was of course also an ideological dimension to this campaign. Specifically, European administrators disapproved strongly of the independence and the power which beer brewing gave some women. In their eyes, all Africans should be subordinate, but women above all, not merely to themselves but also to their menfolk. This could be couched in terms of an attack on the immorality engendered by the shebeens, not recognising that the root cause of such immorality lay in the system which they represented. More generally, particularly after 1948, they saw the towns as places where Africans could only be tolerated in so far as, and as long as, they worked for the whites.

This assault was not confined to liquor sellers. In a whole variety of spheres measures were taken to restrict small-scale African entrepreneurship in places which were not considered desirable. In central Johannesburg and in many other cities, until the early 1960s black workers could purchase tea, coffee, bread and so forth from black-owned carts and permanent kiosks. These replaced small eating houses

6.5 (*cont.*)

1970s and 1980s from radical youth who saw drinking as an unwarranted abrogation from the struggle. By the mid-1990s, however, shebeens might be seen as an integral and important part of South African culture, even being advertised in the tourist guides to Pretoria.

specifically for an African clientele. From then on, this branch of enterprise was suppressed with the loss of livelihood for over 2,000 cart and kiosk owners in Johannesburg alone. Until the 1980s, African hawkers in the central business districts were resolutely suppressed, in the name of hygiene, the preservation of white competitive advantage and, latterly, the fear of 'terrorism'. Equally, small-scale manufacturing, such as furniture-making, panel-beating and so forth, was outlawed from 'white' areas. Spatial constraints and the provision of credit made competition with white industries from the townships more or less impossible, except for products, such as burglar bars and wood-burners, the markets for which were almost entirely among the blacks (at least at this stage). Again, black-run transport networks, notably minibus taxi services, were subjected to continual harassment, to the benefit of white-owned transportation companies in cahoots with the Bantustan rulers.

In the long term, the strategies for the maintenance of white rule through apartheid could not match the strategies for survival among its victims. By the end of the 1980s, the primarily black informal economy provided about a twentieth, at least, of the country's Gross Domestic Product. It provided an income for at least half of those formally considered to be unemployed, and this income exceeded that earned by black mine-workers. Over half of those so engaged were hawkers and petty traders, a quarter were engaged in small-scale manufacturing, about an eighth in various service industries and the rest in activities which other countries as well as South Africa would have considered criminal. By this stage there had been a considerable degree of deregulation, which resulted in many bloody struggles for the control of the newly liberalised economic activities. In the taxi business, in particular, rival groups slaughtered each other, and each other's customers, to acquire monopolies. All the same, the legacy of decades of repression and harassment was a lasting malformation and underdevelopment of a major part of the country's economy, to the detriment of all its inhabitants.

This point can be made more widely. Apartheid worked to the benefit of employers of unskilled, undifferentiated labour. At the same time, it did not encourage – perhaps it even made impossible – an efficient use of labour. South Africa managed to become at once a country of low real wages and one of relatively high labour costs. In particular the location of plant well away from the segregated dormitory suburbs, a consequence of the segregation of space essential to apartheid, forced workers to pay highly purely to get to work. Equally, the deficient infrastructure in the townships, let alone in the informal settlements, forced their inhabitants to pay over the odds for water, heating and light. Poor households not attached to the electricity grid, or unable to pay the connection costs and the running expenses, actually spent as much, absolutely, on energy as those living in the much larger white-owned houses in the same town, or they had to waste much time, and lay waste the environment, by cutting wood. These were costs that were paid, eventually, grudgingly and not in full, by their employers. Again, in a situation of latent or actual conflict, employers were not investing in the training of their workforce, and workers had no reason other than the fear of dismissal to exert themselves. The costs were then those of low productivity.

Productivity was not merely a question of motivation but also of education. Apartheid destroyed the old system of mission education, which provided a high level of education for a tiny elite but also attained something approaching mass literacy in a few select areas. It also inculcated political values which were common to the political class of all backgrounds, and the ending of apartheid was only just in time to allow people still brought up in this tradition the chance to bind the country together again. In the place of the liberal paternalism of the mission schools, the government provided a mass education of a quality that was nearly useless to the modern world.

The basic statistics are clear. Of the 200,000 African children who entered school in 1950, 362 (less than two per thousand) passed matriculation, the qualification for university entrance, twelve years later. Thereafter, the number of secondary schools for Africans increased somewhat, though as we have seen the new schools tended to be located for ideological reasons in the Bantustans, forcing potential scholars to board with relatives, or at school. Funding remained abysmal. In the mid-1970s the government provided R41.80 for each black schoolchild, just 6.5 per cent of the amount granted to each white scholar. In the course of the next decade, this percentage increased to just under twenty. Most African children went to school for a while, but over half left after at most four years of schooling, when they were still, at best, semi-literate. School classes were vast, with a teacher:pupil ratio in primary schools of one to forty-four in 1988. The teachers themselves

6.6 A Black school near Durban in the 1980s, illustrating the
overcrowded conditions of many educational establishments.

were ill-trained; only just over half had the minimum necessary educational qualification. Often, moreover, they were working a double shift
so as to accommodate the maximum number of pupils, albeit at a
minimum level.

In these circumstances, the only strategy for both teachers and pupils
was to eschew any form of independence of mind or analytical think-
ing in favour of rote learning, enforced by a discipline based on the cane.
In this way, they had a chance of sliding through to give themselves a
better chance on the job market. However, subjects which were not
amenable to such learning methods were avoided, in part because the
teachers themselves were not able to cope with them. Thus, even by the
1990s there were scarcely more than 200 Africans a year who passed
mathematics at matriculation level. This was not the way to create a
dynamic labour force.

At the same time, independence of mind could not be eliminated.
Rather, by default, it was channelled into political action. A generation
of children spent their youths challenging the political system under the
slogan 'Liberation Now! Education Later!' Perhaps it was necessary,
and it was certainly understandable, but the costs, among the genuine
costs of apartheid, were enormous.

7

'Let freedom reign': the ending of apartheid and the transition to democracy, 1980–1994

In retrospect, the tendencies which were to lead to the abandonment of apartheid from 1990 were already evident in the late 1970s. At the time, of course, things were not so clear, and these developments were seen as signs of hope by apartheid's opponents, or, by its supporters, as problems which had to be confronted and overcome, if they were recognised at all.

In 1978, John Vorster resigned as Prime Minister of South Africa, to take up the still ceremonial office of President. In part, this resignation was the consequence of his ill-health and exhaustion, in part to avoid the consequences of financial scandals with which he was implicated (though he probably did not himself profit). In the hope of containing the attacks on the country, Vorster had sanctioned the accumulation of unsupervised resources in the hands of various secret bodies charged with making propaganda for the government. The unchecked power a few men thus acquired had its usual corrupting, and aphrodisiac, effect. The scandal leaked out slowly, to the Cabinet, the Press and Nationalist members of Parliament, ensuring both Vorster's fall and, in the elections to determine the new Prime Minister, the defeat of Connie Mulder, who was expected to be the successor, at the hands of P.W. Botha.

Botha was a fearsome man even by the standards of Nationalist politicians, well meriting his nickname 'The Great Crocodile'. He was of the type who reacted to any form of pressure by affirming his own position with greater force. He differed in two significant respects from

7.1 P.W. Botha in his element at an army review.

those he ousted. He was the head of the National Party in the Cape
Province, whereas his opponents were Transvaalers, and as Minister of
Defence his power base within the Government was with the army,
whereas Vorster had cultivated links with the police, and with the security agencies such as BOSS which indeed he had created. As it happened,
both of these characteristics accorded with important developments
within the South African body politic.

To begin with the latter, during the course of the 1980s, the militar-
isation of South African politics proceeded apace. Using their connection with Botha, the leadership of the South African Defence Force,
notably its head General Magnus Malan, began to propagate the programme known as 'Total Strategy'. They were convinced that South
Africa was the target of a total assault by Communism under the leadership of the Soviet Union. They saw the ANC merely as the minions of
Moscow. Now, there were several Communists in leading positions particularly in *Umkhonto we Siswe*, the ANC's armed wing. Joe Slovo, of
Lithuanian extraction, and Chris Hani, from the Transkei, the two most
notable of these men, became white South Africa's greatest devils. The
ANC also received funding from the Soviet Union, as well as from many
Western countries. Moreover, the stress on the Communist threat to
South Africa found a sympathetic hearing in Reaganite Washington,

where the pressure on South Africa imposed by the Carter administration declined after 1980. However, in general, the South African government's obsession with the dangers of Communism only served to increase support for the South African Communist Party.

Total strategy had two main components. The first was more strictly military. The threat had to be contained as far beyond South Africa's borders as possible. It had proved impossible by 1980 to prevent the old Portuguese colonies and Zimbabwe from being ruled, in theory, by the ANC's allies. The South Africans therefore attempted to emasculate these countries in various covert ways. Their success in Zimbabwe was limited, but in Mozambique their creation, RENAMO, waged a dirty civil war which reduced the country to ruins. In Angola, the South Africans also kept the war going, while at the same time turning Ovamboland in northern Namibia, the region where most of that country's population lives, into a fortress to prevent infiltration.

Many of these operations were necessarily conducted in secrecy, as was their continuation within South Africa, where various branches of the military were involved in assassinations and in building up private armies to act within the political struggle. In consequence, it is questionable how far they remained under the control of their political commanders, and how far they began to act on their own account. Their political actions could run beyond what was permitted, and certainly what was explicitly sanctioned, and their power could give them opportunities for self-enrichment, notably through the drugs and ivory trade.

The second component of Total Strategy was more strictly political. The argument was that the achievement of legitimacy and consensus was an essential for the containment of Communism. This intermeshed with Botha's other major underpinning, namely the Cape Nationalist Party, within which capitalist companies, notably SANLAM, had far more influence than within the ideologically far purer Transvaal Party. These sorts of nationalists did not reject the basic assumptions or methods of apartheid. If they had, they would have left the National Party. They merely recognised that some degree of economic and social reform was necessary in order to maintain Afrikaner supremacy and white prosperity.

Ultimately, the problems were insoluble, and by the end of the 1980s were recognised to be so. In order to survive, apartheid would have had to have reconciled two prime contradictions. It would have had to adapt a social and economic system predicated on the labour-intensive exploitation of a mass and unskilled black labour force to the increasingly capital-intensive requirements of the late twentieth century. Even in the gold mines, the proportion of blacks in unskilled jobs fell from 68 per cent in 1960 to 53 per cent two decades later. Workers could no longer be seen as infinitely interchangeable units of production. This meant that, despite the atrociously high rate of unemployment, those who were in work had a previously unappreciated degree of power within the workplace.

At the same time, the transition to a somewhat more capital-intensive economy made South Africa more vulnerable to the international economic sanctions half-heartedly imposed on it because of its racial policies. The only significant primary product that the country lacked was oil. However, the oil boycott could be evaded, at a price, and considerable efforts were made to develop technologies for the extraction from South Africa's massive coal deposits of motor fuel and the other goods usually made from oil. It was the decline in the import of capital goods, and in foreign investment, that hit the country far harder. Here sanctions, and the hard-headed calculation that such investments were too high a risk, significantly impeded the growth of the South African economy. In July 1985, Chase Manhattan bank decided that political unrest in the country meant that it was too risky to roll over loans to its South African debtors, and many other banks followed suit. Self-fulfilling prophecy as such actions are, it thereby exacerbated the economic crisis.

The second contradiction was political. The apartheid state would somehow have had to increase its legitimacy and its political base without compromising its essential character. The aim was to find a way of 'sharing power while retaining control', as it was put at the time. Without this, it was to prove impossible both to contain black unrest and to shed the status of international pariah that the country had acquired. Its formal racial discrimination now entailed the exclusion of the country from participation in the world order. This led to the imposition of sanctions, both economic, with long-term debilitating effects, and in other ways. The most important of these was on the sports fields. Particularly the suspension of international rugby matches was a heavy psychological blow to the Afrikaners, who were accustomed to demonstrating their superiority through their sporting prowess.

7.2 Rugby was introduced into South Africa in the late
nineteenth century through the English-speaking private church
schools. It quickly spread to all communities, at least in the Cape
Colony. In Cape Town, Kimberley and the Eastern Cape black
and coloured clubs soon developed. Cape Town's Muslims took
up the game, often as much as spectators and supporters of the
whites than as players. One legendary white player always
carried a Muslim charm onto the field with him, and was injured
when he forgot it. As with cricket, it also became a marker of the
mission-educated black elite, particularly in the Eastern Cape.
These people have continued to play the sport, often under
wretched conditions. Steve Tshwete, now Minister of Sport, even
organised a rugby competition while a prisoner on Robben
Island.

    Nevertheless, it was among the Afrikaners that Rugby
achieved its greatest popularity. The country diet had given many
Afrikaners the physique with which to impose themselves in this
most size-sensitive of games. From the 1920s, South African
international teams, known as the Springboks, shown here
playing Australia, were usually dominant, and as they were
predominantly made up of Afrikaners were seen as an index of
that group's power. At a more local level, rugby provided an
opportunity for the manifestation of a rawness and brutality
which was central to the self-image of many white South African
males as males.

Through the early 1980s attempts were made to reform the South African system in piecemeal ways that would not affect its essential character. In 1979 and 1981, the Government held high-profile conferences with business leaders in an attempt to win their support for the new course. At the same time, it instituted a number of commissions to advise it on crucial matters of policy. Thus the Wiehahn commission on industrial labour recommended the recognition of black trade unions, the abolition of the statutory job colour bar and the opening of apprenticeships to Africans. From 1979, these measures were implemented. In consequence, through the early 1980s black unions were formed in high tempo. At least initially, most concentrated purely on industrial matters. They did not want their actions subordinated to what they saw as the political agendas of the middle class, both for fear of their suppression if they were too overtly 'political' and to maximise the benefits they could obtain for their members. All the same the conglomerates, the Federation of South African Trade Unions (FOSATO) and the Council of Unions of South Africa (CUSA), were for a time the largest black organisations in the country (except for some churches). Out of CUSA, which demanded black working-class leadership, was formed the National Union of Mineworkers (NUM), organising among the underground migrant labourers in the aftermath of a major unofficial strike on the gold mines in 1982. Its Secretary-General, Cyril Ramaphosa, a university graduate from Venda in the far north Transvaal, was to acquire in the Union the skills which made him one of the most astute and effective negotiators in the country.

The two other main government commissions of the early 1980s were those chaired by P.J. Riekert on manpower utilisation and by J.P. de Lange on education. The latter recognised the need to improve the standard of black education and to equalise the government subsidies between the races, but balked both at the cost of these measures and at the threat to grand apartheid which they represented. The former attempted to widen the privileges of those Africans who had acquired the right to live in one of the cities. These provisions were not always welcomed, or applied, by the mass of bureaucrats whose jobs depended on the old order to which they had learnt to give ideological commitment. Although the measures would not imply full South African citizenship, they did mean that there was to be a certain amount of autonomy for the black townships. The authorities so created had to be self-supporting, financially, and thus to collect rents and local taxes, a considerable source of tension. On the other hand, those who did not have such rights were to be even more rigorously barred from migration to the cities. The distinction between 'insiders' and 'outsiders' was thus further entrenched, only adding to the risk of urban conflagration.

This piecemeal, unconvinced reform programme was based on the government's realisation that it could no longer maintain its power without building up alliances among its subjects. The legislation proposed by the Riekert and, to some extent, the Wiehahn commissions was expected to make the urban Africans it privileged feel bounden to the government. P.W. Botha's 1985 visit to the celebration of Easter at Moria, the headquarters of the Zion Christian Church, the largest independent church in the country, was an expression of the same strategy. Its most important element was constitutional. In 1984, following a commission headed by Alwyn Schlebusch, the government inaugurated a new constitution for the country. This was a typical example of both its authoritarianism and its half-heartedness. On the one hand it concentrated power in the President's council, elevating the President of the country from the figurehead he had been since the proclamation of the Republic in 1961 to an almost monarchical ruler of the country. P.W. Botha, naturally enough, moved from being Prime Minister to the Presidency. On the other, it for the first time gave the coloureds and Indians a formal say in the ruling of the country through a tricameral parliament. The majority parties in their parliaments could nominate a number of members to the Council, but in such numbers that they would always be in a minority as against those nominated by the majority party – in effect, though not in law, the National Party – in the white parliament. Africans remained rigorously excluded. After all, so went the theory, they could exercise their rights through the Bantustans, of which four were independent states and the others moving in that direction. Even National Party ideologues had failed to make the concept of a 'homeland' for coloureds and Indians, away from the whites, at all plausible.

This constitution was accepted after a referendum among the white voters, by a majority of about two to one. It did however produce very considerable opposition. It provided the hard right within even more evidence that Botha was abandoning true Verwoerdian principles, and strengthened their hand against the National Party. To the left, there were vehement protests against the constitution and against the so-called Koornhof bills by which Piet Koornhof as minister for Co-operation and Development (as the Bantu Affairs Department had been renamed in late-apartheid doublespeak) attempted to implement the recommendations of the Riekert commission. These protests led directly to the foundation of the United Democratic Front, which was to prove the largest and most effective movement of opposition to apartheid.

The UDF was a front in two senses. Certainly it saw itself as representing the banned ANC. It saw the Freedom Charter as the basis of its programme. At its head were twenty patrons, largely of Congress background and including a number of men still on Robben Island. Its three presidents, Archie Gumede, Oscar Mpetha and Albertina Sisulu, were all veterans of Congress campaigns in the 1950s. Its executive committee, on the other hand, was made up of younger activists, of wide background (although few members had much experience in Trade Union organisation) and generally skilled in the manipulation of the media.

The UDF was also a front in that it consisted of several hundred affiliated organisations, which were generally locally based action groups. Typically, there would be a civic organisation, a women's organisation and a youth group in the various townships and, increasingly, in the bantustans. There were also a number of religious organisations, strictly political groups, such as the Release Mandela campaign, and one or two newspapers which affiliated. Initially, there were few Trade Unions, but after 1985 FOSATU and various community-based unions united in the Congress of South African Trade Unions (COSATU) which worked in alliance with the UDF. In consequence, although the UDF top was able to organise a number of concerted campaigns, the Front's strength derived from the local issues around which the various affiliates were able to mobilise, and also from the fact that the arrest of the leaders by the government did not paralyse mass activity. On the other hand, neither the national leadership nor the ANC in exile in Lusaka was able to exercise much control over what was going on, and was on occasion horrified by actions associated with the UDF.

In November 1984, the UDF's protests particularly against rent collection and the new black local authorities erupted into open revolt, initially in the Vaal townships of Sebokeng and Sharpeville around Vereeniging to the south of Johannesburg. From there the revolt spread.

Its main foci were in the Eastern Cape, where by early 1986 twenty-seven townships were said to be under UDF/ANC control, in the industrial heartland of what later came to be known as Gauteng (Pretoria, the Witwatersrand and the Vaal triangle), in greater Cape Town and in some of the Bantustans of the Transvaal, but there were few areas of the country which were untouched. It was retrospectively legitimated by the ANC in Lusaka calling for the country to be made ungovernable.

As in all such uprisings, the main participants were the 'youth', particularly the young men. To some extent, this is a tautological comment. 'Youth' was defined not merely by age, but also by political activism. Against this, the combination of widespread education, with which the pupils were in general rightly dissatisfied, and almost total unemployment among school-leavers meant that there was a wide constituency eager to answer the call for political activism when it came. The culture of resistance, with its Freedom songs, *toyi-toyi* dancing and stone-throwing, was thrilling. The various local and regional Youth Congresses which joined together in the South African Youth Congress under the leadership of Robben Island graduate Peter Mokaba thus represented the most radical and militant elements within the revolt.

It was always a question how far these groups of 'youth' were under the control, or at least under the restraint, of the fully adult. The impatient activism of youth was balanced precariously against the respect for age with which they had been brought up, particularly as that respect might no longer be justified. The internal political history of many African communities through the 1980s revolved around this matter. There were certainly areas in which the balance held. One example would be Kagiso, a black suburb of Krugersdorp on the West Rand. Superficially, it seemed relatively quiescent. Nevertheless, the Residents' Organisation in alliance with the local Trade Unions effectively took control of the township for a couple of years. The local authorities set up under the Koornhof bills were unable to function. Kagiso participated in the boycotting of local supermarkets and bus firms, as blacks attempted to use their economic power as consumers to exert pressure for political change. 'Youth' imposed this boycott on the Kagiso residents, but in so doing the force they used was restrained. There were no political executions. Rather, as in many other places, a system of informal but effective local justice emerged by which local notables ensured that the social norms were enforced, the strains on township life not-

7.3 The Conga-like *toyi-toyi* dance of the 'youth' at UDF and other 'radical' gatherings during the 1980s was at once a metaphor for the unifying aspirations of the Front and a potent psychological means of achieving that solidarity, at least among the participants. In this, it had its roots in pre-colonial war dances. Through the earlier part of the twentieth century, such withstanding. This was the work of the leaders within the community, notably Sister Bernard Ncube, a nun living in Kagiso. The 'youth' was quite prepared to hand over responsibility for such matters to those seen as settled enough to exercise it.

As a nun and thus outside the structures of familial gender authority, Sister Bernard was perhaps able to act in ways closed off to most women, even though she in no way denied the fact of her womanhood, and had indeed been President of the Federation of Transvaal Women. The particular history of Kagiso, where the youth movement had grown out of Christian fellowships, had made her rise to a position of leadership easier. All the same, as a Christian leader within the UDF, she was thoroughly typical. Many of the most prominent leaders of the opposition at the time were committed, often ordained, Christians. Beyers Naudé, Allan Boesak, both ministers of the Dutch Reformed Church (the former white, the latter coloured) and the Anglican Archbishop of Cape Town, Desmond Tutu, were perhaps the most eminent of these, but their message was one which found wide resonance. They could give expression to the widespread belief that opposition was a moral duty, within a morality which had been first propagated by the missionaries and over nearly two centuries adopted and internalised very widely within the country.

Kagiso was not an exceptional place. Its experience through the turbulent 1980s was in many ways ordinary. Nevertheless, it did not represent the only pattern through which black communities passed. Despite the exertions of men like Tutu, and to the dismay of many in the leadership of the UDF and the ANC in exile, there were many places where the 'struggle' became murderous. Those who remained 'within the system' as policemen or local councillors, or those alleged to have been informers for the government, ran a considerable risk of being hacked to death, or more formally executed by 'necklacing'. In this, a way of purging the community of evil, a car tyre was placed around the victim's neck, filled with petrol and set on fire.

7.3 (cont.)
transformations of dance forms were most often performed by migrant workers in the mine compounds, and often took on a folkloristic character while at the same time confirming the local, often ethnic, identities of the miners.

(1)   (2)   (3)   (4)

7.4 Four church leaders whose activities went beyond the confines of their domination: Dr J.D. Vorster, of the *Nederlands Gereformeerde Kerk*, who held the hard line of apartheid for his brother, John (1); Dr Beyers Naudé, who came to see the incompatibility of apartheid and the Calvinist faith in which he remained, and departed from the heart of Afrikanerdom to found the Christian Institute and give hope to many questioning Christians, black and white (2); Desmond Tutu, Anglican Archbishop of Cape Town, who exploited the inviolability of his position and his personal reputation for integrity to attack both the injustices of apartheid and the excesses of the struggle against it – after 1994 he would remain crucial as chairman of the Truth and Reconciliation Committee (3); the Rev. Frank Chikane, minister of the Apostolic Faith Mission in Kagiso, by Krugersdorp, and a leading figure both in the Institute for Contextual Theology, which was concerned with developing South African theologies of liberation, and in the UDF in the Transvaal (4).

The control which the militant young men held over black communities could lead to further excesses when not tempered either by sufficient political education or by sympathetic elders. Such young men
could be used to build up the personal power bases of individuals, many
of whom professed allegiance to the UDF and ANC. Nelson Mandela's
wife Winnie was the most notorious of these, but by no means the only
one. By the late 1980s, however, her personal rule in part of Soweto had
turned murderous. The UDF and ANC attempted unsuccessfully to rein
her in, and the Government decided to tolerate her actions, so as to dis-
credit the Mandela name. In a number of areas, the loss of life to
government repression resulted in the 'Making Soldiers' campaign. To
ensure that, eventually, the government would be overwhelmed by the
force of numbers, all young women had to become pregnant within a
year. The 'youth' set about ensuring this with a will.

The events in Sekhukhuneland in the Northern Transvaal were particularly dramatic. The area, declared part of the Lebowa Bantustan,
was becoming drastically impoverished, and contained a large number
of unemployed young men whose hope of finding work was greatly
diminished by the decline in migrant labour in Johannesburg. It also
had a long tradition of resistance, exemplified by the Sebatakgomo
movement in the 1950s, and had been the short-lived focus of an MK
guerrilla incursion led by Gabriel 'Tokyo' Sexwale, later the premier of
Gauteng. The presence of Peter Nchabaleng, a Robben Island graduate
and Congress stalwart, with his sons, gave a degree of direction to the
movement which emerged in a number of villages. It was aimed essentially at the Lebowa government officials, who were correctly seen as the
minions of Pretoria. However, a number of accidents which the
Sekhukhuneland 'comrades' suffered convinced many of them that they
were afflicted by witchcraft. Nchabaleng, who was to be murdered in
police custody, did his best to restrain the 'youth', but without success.
In a few months in early 1986, some thirty-six people were burned to
death as witches in the villages of Nkwana and Appel, the kernel of the
revolt. The average age of the victims was over sixty; that of their exe-
cutioners, nineteen.

Two points need to be made about this shocking episode. First,
alleged witches had regularly been done to death in pre-colonial times,
and the ideas of maleficence which had justified this have survived and
developed through the twentieth century. Indeed, there are indications

7.5 In pre-colonial South Africa people's bodies and the objects they used were beautified, often with the beads which were among the major trade goods of Europeans. There was also a tradition of decorating houses, which in the twentieth century was extended by the women of the Ndzundza Ndebele in the Northern Province to mark their communal identity with striking multi-coloured geometric wall paintings. However, the objects which were produced were in general of the type which Europeans would characterize as 'ethnographica' and were not transformable into that contextless and functionless universality long thought necessary for 'art'.

There was one major exception to this. In the Northern province there was a tradition of figurative wood-carving. Among the Balovedu, carved poles were used to surround the *kgôrô*, the centre of political authority, as a sign of royal, in this case queenly, power. In Venda, too, doors, drums and other objects were carved with bas-reliefs, and clay and wooden figurines were used as teaching aids in the girls' initation schools.

At various periods, the skills developed in these contexts were exploited for the production of 'art' for the market. Wooden sculptures were made near Pretoria for sale to visitors from the 1890s. More recently, a number of sculptors have begun to produce works of great power, in a medium of painted wood. This has proved dangerous, as they have been accused not merely that the concentration of people in the Bantustans, particularly in the Transvaal, and the consequent increase in interpersonal tensions, meant that more people were suspected of witchcraft, often with fatal results. Leading Bantustan politicians, particularly in Venda, were thought to be using sorcery for political ends. However, since the state did not recognise the reality of witchcraft, and indeed made it an offence to accuse someone of being a witch – and was therefore seen at some times and in some places as the protector of witches, and as deriving its own power from the occult – these accusations remained simmering, and no methods were discovered for purging the whole community of the evil. Secondly, the circumstances of the mass killings in 1986, and indeed the general upsurge in witchcraft accusations, resemble those in many such outbreaks, particularly in seventeenth-century Europe and in North America, in an absence of a strong and respected structure of authority able to check the rumours at source and prevent the movement from spreading. The long-term decline in chiefly legitimacy, especially after the chiefs had been coopted into the Bantustan government, and the temporary break-down of political order in the summer of 1985–6 help explain the events in question. At the very least, respected village government would have ensured that the youth went through the correct procedures, consulting diviners and so forth, before killing the alleged witches.

Not all the struggles even in the rural Transvaal led to such excesses. Widespread protests defeated the proposed incorporation of the largely Sotho enclave of Moutswe into Kwandebele and the independence of the latter Bantustan. In this case, the combination of 'youth', both from the area itself and from Pretoria, for which Kwandebele had become a long-distance commuter suburb, and the Ndebele royal family was decisive against the government-sponsored Chief Minister of Kwandebele, S.S. Skosana, and his personal private army, known as Mbodoko.

In working through Skosana and Mbodoko, the South African government was following a tactic which it used widely throughout the

7.5 (*cont.*)
of betraying the secrets of the initiation, but also of witchcraft, and of using the images to turn their neighbours into zombies. The wealth which they acquired from sales to European and South African collectors gave credence to this belief, which resulted in a number of cases in their execution.

1980s. On the one hand, the revolt associated with the UDF brought about a temporary end to the reform process of the early Botha years and a massive increase in direct repression. The proclamation of a State of Emergency, initially in selected districts (though covering a very large proportion of the population) and then in June 1986 throughout the country signalled the entrenchment of the security forces and the securocrats as the true rulers of South Africa and gave them great powers. The widespread shootings of demonstrators and the calculated assassination of prominent opponents at first only inflamed the revolt. The funerals of those so killed became great political rallies. By early 1988, when the UDF and sixteen other organisations were formally banned, however, terror had done its work, and the revolt had been crushed.

On the other hand, this victory for the forces of repression was only possible because the government was able to recruit considerable numbers of blacks to do part of its dirty work for it. Auxiliary police, known as *kitskonstabels* because their lack of training made it seem as if they were assembled from pre-fabricated kits, were deployed widely. Less officially, squads of vigilantes under the control of local warlords took it upon themselves to smash the 'comrades' movement in many black townships.

While this process occurred throughout the country, including, as we have seen, in the squatter settlements around Cape Town, it grew to its most serious proportions in Natal. In the course of the 1980s, the conflict between Chief Buthelezi's Inkatha Freedom Party and the UDF grew into a full-scale civil war in which several thousand people were killed.

The roots of the conflict can be traced back a hundred and fifty years to the divide between the Zulu Kingdom north of the Thukela river and the colony of Natal to the south. In Zululand proper, chiefly authority survived, or more strictly was periodically recreated, to a degree that was never the case further south. This authority was strengthened by the prevalence of migrant labour in the area, as the men away from home relied on the chiefly structures to preserve their rights over land and over their womenfolk. This, coupled with a skilled use of the symbols of Zulu ethnic nationalism and his encapsulation and exploitation of the Zulu royal family, allowed Buthelezi to acquire a legitimacy for his rule as Bantustan leader far in excess of that enjoyed by any of his fellows. Once in power, he was able to exploit the all-per-

vading poverty of Zululand to ensure adherence to the Inkatha movement which he led, and to the government of KwaZulu, through a combination of patronage and the repression of opposition. His followers
indeed came to see themselves as the successors to the *impi*s of the nineteenth century. Their participation within Inkatha was thus an integral
part of their manly identity.

These were not considerations which weighed heavily with the urban
inhabitants of Durban and Pietermaritzburg, and of the slums which
stretched out between the two original colonial cities. In common with
their fellows across the Republic, they were more attracted to the UDF.
They spoke Zulu as their first language, and might have described themselves as Zulu, but it was not the identity to which they adhered, and for
which they were prepared to die. In this, a tradition of Charterist politics and a widespread membership of COSATU-affiliated trade unions
both played their part.

The war in Natal was a long series of murders, revenge killings, the
burning of huts and the driving of women and children out of informal
settlements. It was driven on by ideas of Zuluness which only became
strong as the conflict continued and was fanned by government security forces as a way of weakening the UDF. At its root, though, it was a
struggle for political territory. The UDF potentially threatened Inkatha
control over KwaZulu, and thereby endangered not merely the political
position of the leaders but also the sources of their patronage system.
The poverty of their followers meant that this was a system for whose
preservation they were prepared to fight.

The suppression of the township revolt by late 1987 and the banning
of the UDF shifted the emphasis of the general conflict in Southern
Africa in two directions. The first was in the field of trade unionism.
Despite the massive unemployment of the 1980s, and thus in theory the
greater power of management as against the workforce, there was an
upsurge in union activity. It would seem as though those who had a job
were using union activity in an attempt to safeguard their position. At
the same time, the changing characteristics of the labour demand in the
country meant that African workers could no longer be seen as infinitely interreplaceable units of production. In particular, the National
Union of Mineworkers succeeded in organising the great majority of
migrant labourers, historically the most vulnerable and difficult to
unionise group of workers. In 1987, the NUM both declared its alle-

giance to the ANC, making Nelson Mandela its honourary life president, and called a total strike of the gold mines over wages. The strike
was defeated, and large numbers of workers lost their jobs, at least temporarily, but the solidarity they and their fellows in many other industries demonstrated the power, both industrial and political, which the
unions possessed.

The second main locus of conflict was beyond the borders of the
Republic. Total Strategy was predicated upon the existence of a Total
Onslaught on South Africa. Armed incursions into South Africa had to
be stopped at source, and the line held. Only in this way, it was believed,
could peace and political development be ensured in the country. From
the point of view of the South African securocrats, the result was disastrous. The government was able to destabilise Mozambique and in
1984 impose the humiliating Nkomati accord on its FRELIMO government under Samora Machel, but this did not end the war there. It was
also able to force the ANC to relinquish its forward bases in Zambia,
thereby strengthening the hand of those within the organisation who
were arguing for a negotiated settlement. In Angola, in contrast, it was
sucked ever deeper into the slough of conflict by its support for Jonas
Savimbi's UNITA movement. In the summer of 1987–8, a substantial
force of the South African army first defeated the Angolans in the battle
of Lomba river and then laid seige to the strategic town of Cuito
Cuanavale in South Central Angola. To relieve the town, the Angolans
brought up Cuban troops, who were paid for out of the taxes levied on
the American company Gulf Oil for their exploitation of the Cabinda
oil fields. For the first time, the effects of the weapons boycott on South
Africa made themselves felt. Its outdated Mirage fighters were driven
out of the sky by Russian-made MIGs. White battalions began to
mutiny, and the army was outflanked and forced to retreat to the
Cunene, leaving behind all its heavy equipment. Its annihilation was a
real possibility, but instead the Cubans enforced South African agreement to the United Nations Resolution calling for the independence of
Namibia. South African attempts to influence the subsequent elections
so as to produce an acceptable government failed, and in 1990 seventy-
five years of South African rule came to an end. The South West African
People's Organisation, an ally of the ANC, took over.

The rise of the UDF had the concomitant effect of sharply increasing
the profile of the ANC. Many of the leading activists in the UDF were

themselves clandestine members of the ANC and the Front saw the Freedom Charter as the basis of its action. The influence of the exiled ANC on internal political developments became greater than it had been since 1960. Leading ANC members, notably Mac Maharaj, entered the country and acted not as guerrillas but as counsellors. For the first time, prominent white intellectuals and businessmen began to make their way to Lusaka or elsewhere, for discussions with the ANC top, and were surprised, and somewhat relieved, by what they met. An organisation whose President, Oliver Tambo, said grace before dinner could not be as devilish as it had been portrayed within South Africa. The government condemned these meetings in public, although it clearly had its channels to find out what was discussed. At the same time, it opened cautious and mutually deniable discussions with the African National Congress, both with the exiles and with Nelson Mandela, who by this time had been brought from Robben Island, first to Pollsmoor in the suburbs of Cape Town and then to Victor Verster Prison in the winelands near Paarl. These latter contacts had been initiated by the Minister of Justice, and Mandela's nominal gaoler, Kobie Coetsee. The government was thus playing a double game, and probably only P.W. Botha knew the details of both its actions against the ANC, including the arming of Inkatha and vigilante groups, and of its negotiations.

In January 1989, P.W. Botha had a mild stroke. Within a month, still in hospital, he decided to cut down on his commitments by relinquishing the leadership of the National Party while remaining State President. Whatever his political calculations in taking this act may have been, they went wrong. By a small majority, the party caucus in Parliament elected F.W. De Klerk as its new leader. De Klerk, a mild-mannered conciliator from the Transvaal and once a brilliant academic lawyer, was a nephew of Prime Minister Hans Strijdom and the son of a former candidate for the State Presidency. He was thus a man from the heart of Afrikanerdom, and seen as being on the right of the Party.

For the rest of 1989, South Africa marked time. The division between the Presidency and the leadership of the Party meant that neither Botha nor De Klerk could exercise real power. De Klerk, though, could begin to dismantle the power of the Securocrats, notably Magnus Malan, an old family enemy. In September, however, elections were held, in which the National Party retained Parliamentary power, though losing seats to

7.6 F.W. De Klerk

the far right, and De Klerk was elected President, Botha having been forced to stand down.

After the elections, De Klerk released from prison many of the leading ANC figures, notably Walter Sisulu and Ahmed Kathrada. Govan Mbeki, the oldest of the Rivonia trialists, had indeed been let out two and a half years earlier, and publicly reaffirmed his membership of the ANC and the Communist Party. Then, when Parliament reconvened on 2 February 1990, De Klerk announced that the bans on the ANC, the South African Communist Party, the Pan-African Congress and all other proscribed organisations were to be lifted forthwith. Nine days later, Nelson Mandela walked out of Victor Verster prison and was driven to Cape Town, where he addressed a massive crowd from the balcony of the Town Hall. A tall, stately, grey-haired man who had never seen a television camera, his release after twenty-seven years in gaol provided some of the most moving images the medium has seen, and signalled the genuine beginning of the process of transition by which South Africa could start to rid itself of its apartheid past.

Why did De Klerk, and the cabinet with him, take the measures they did? It is after all not that common for a ruling group to change the rules under which it maintains power other than under duress, and the ANC was a long way from storming the government buildings in Pretoria. There was an alternative – continued repression – by which the government could probably have held on to power for another decade or so. But this was not an option which De Klerk and those around him were prepared to take. Obviously, long-term historical trends were at work. The original impetus of Afrikaner nationalism had disappeared. The British Empire had long ceased to be a bogey, and, if Afrikaners were not on average as wealthy as South Africa's English-speaking whites, the differentials were no longer so great that this was a major issue. However, the stagnation, and indeed decline, of the South African economy were putting this white prosperity in jeopardy. Radical solutions had to be found, which could only come with political reform.

In the somewhat shorter term, the unrest of the 1980s had taken its toll. The revolt in the townships and Reserves had been defeated, and no doubt could be again. Despite the retreat from Namibia, the threats from the north, or from ANC guerrillas, were not challenging to the core of the South African state. Both, however, were costing too much in money and white lives. They also served to increase international indignation towards, and thus pressure on, South Africa. This had military, economic and moral consequences. The effects of the arms embargo had been seen at Cuito Cuanavale. As a form of defence, the government had always done its utmost to satisfy its international creditors, but they were becoming less accommodating. The trading boycott was squeezing the investment which alone would revitalise the economy. The moral crusade against South Africa was beginning to strike home, and the theological certainties which had sustained apartheid were giving way to criticism, even from within the Reformed churches to which the Afrikaner leadership belonged, in De Klerk's personal case with fervent belief.

Finally, the collapse of Communist rule in eastern Europe, symbolised by the fall of the Berlin Wall in November 1989, changed Afrikaner perceptions of their opponents and themselves. They could no longer claim to be the bastions of Christian civilisation against the hordes of the evil empire, a perception which their contacts with the ANC top had in any event done much to dispel – and the government probably calculated that the withdrawal of Soviet financial support would emasculate

7.7 Four leading writers. B.W. Vilakazi, who as a teacher of
Zulu at the University of the Witwatersrand developed new
forms of Zulu poetry (1); N.P. van Wyk Louw, the finest
Afrikaner poet, a liberal nationalist (as he described himself)
who combined a great feeling for the *taal* with a hatred of those
who made it into an instrument of oppression (2);

the ANC. At the same time, these events meant that lingering American distrust for the ANC as a Communist front, and consequent support for the South African status quo, no longer had any geopolitical rationale.

At all events, there is no doubt that De Klerk and his fellows calculated that they could control the process of transition in such a way as to guarantee their own interests, and probably to maintain their rule. It was to prove a mistaken calculation.

The history of South Africa between February 1990 and April 1994 was chaotic and bloody, though not as bloody as it might have been. It was not a period during which the real problems of South Africa, other than the political and constitutional, could be addressed. Clarity had to be achieved on who would rule the country, in whose interests, and what the administrative and bureaucratic structure of the country would be. These after all were serious enough uncertainties.

Nevertheless, in the immediate aftermath of De Klerk's speech a beginning was made with the dismantling of the Old Order, without as yet anything being erected to be put in its place. The core was the repeal of the Population Registration Act, in 1991. No longer could people claim rights, and more importantly be deprived of them, on the basis of racial or ethnic classification. At the same time, the Group Areas and Natives Land Acts were repealed (the latter being redesignated the Black Lands Act), and a catch-all Abolition of Racially Based Measures Act passed, removing some sixty pieces of legislation. The result was the final breaking of the dam, already leaking heavily, on which the territorial segregation of apartheid was based. Blacks from the hopelessness of the Reserves and the white farms came into the towns, swelling the numbers of informal settlements and back-yard shacks, and increasing the competition for the scarce jobs.

7.7 (cont.)
Alex La Guma, novelist, trades unionist and Communist, who from political exile wrote a number of novels of his native Cape Town with the sharp realism characteristic of most black fiction (3); Nadine Gordimer, novelist and Nobel prize-winner in 1991, whose stories always denote with keen observations the paradoxes and strains of white South African life, seen from the perspective of her white and black characters, and which have on occasion moved in the direction of more experimental forms (4).

On 2 February 1990, De Klerk did not merely legalise a host of previously illegal organisations. He also made it plain that negotiations would start in earnest, and in public, to create a new political order. Three matters are of great importance in trying to understand the complicated process over the next years. First, one absolute, almost unspoken, requirement was constitutional continuity. Whatever was to be agreed was to be enacted by the South African Parliament, and the government which came out of the process of transition was to be in all respects the lawful successor of the one which went into that process. This most salutary stress on the rule of law had an important political consequence. The process had to be completed within five years, the lifetime of the South African Parliament, as otherwise new elections would have had to be held under the old dispensation, which would certainly have been a major embarrassment to the De Klerk government. The pressure of time came to weigh heavily on the National Party negotiators.

Secondly, except for the Democratic party, the successor to the Progressive Federal Party of the old white parliament, all the groups involved in the process of negotiations coupled the use of force to their bargaining. Everyone had their own private, clandestine army (in addition of course to the government's official defence and police forces), and everyone was prepared to use it as and when they felt necessary or advantageous. The only question was whether or not they could restrain these armies.

Thirdly, in addition to the internal struggles, the course of the negotiations was determined by the close interest which the outside world took in the events in South Africa. Specifically, leverage could be imposed by the decision when to lift economic (and other) sanctions, and thus begin the revitalisation of the economy. In effect, since it had won the propaganda war, the ANC was able to determine when this weapon could be used.

The first months after the lifting of the ban on the ANC were spent organising the return of the exiles and the initial formal meetings. The intelligence communities of both the ANC and the Government met to settle arrangements, in such secrecy that a warrant was issued for the arrest of Jacob Zuma, head of ANC intelligence, while he was staying with the head of the South African secret police. The first significant compromise was reached when the government accepted that Joe Slovo be allowed as a member of the ANC delegation. It was well that they did so, for this portly, jovial Communist turned out to be, not the bogey-man of white fears, but rather the most realistic and hard-headed figure on either side. On two occasions, he made interventions of great moment, which expedited the process very considerably and could probably only have been proposed by someone of his unimpeachable revolutionary credentials. Even Mandela might originally have lost credibility with the radicals; Slovo was above suspicion.

The first such came in August of 1990, when at Slovo's suggestion the ANC unilaterally announced that it was suspending the armed struggle which it had taken up three decades earlier. In practical terms, this meant little. *Umkhonto we Sizwe* was not disbanded and anyway was not able to challenge the might of the South African defence forces. Symbolically, though, it gave the National Party space in which to proceed to genuine negotiations about the future constitution of the country.

It was probably the case that this announcement was just in time. Already, the violence which had racked Natal for years was spreading over the Drakensberg into the townships of the Rand, and within days the low-intensity civil war was claiming hundreds of black lives. There were three interconnected strands to the war, at least on the side of the ANC's opponents. First, Buthelezi and the Inkatha Freedom Party were engaged in consolidating their hold over their fiefdom in KwaZulu-Natal. In this, they received material if clandestine support from at least some of those within the securocrat establishment who were in no way reconciled to the power which the ANC was able to make manifest. Indeed, it was only in 1991 that Magnus Malan finally lost his position within the cabinet, as a result of his secret financing of Inkatha.

Secondly, there were those with the secret forces with a much stronger agenda. They seem to have been attempting to stop the process of nego-tiations in the only way they knew, namely by launching unprovoked and random attacks on blacks, particularly among the commuters on Johannesburg's railway network. It is uncertain precisely what De Klerk had been informed of in this, and even more whether he had the power to restrain his generals. Nevertheless, the suspicion that he had been condoning the massacres, even if only passively, soured the initially good relations between him and Mandela.

Thirdly, the largely Zulu migrant workers who issued from the massive barracks, known as hostels, in the black suburbs of the Rand and murdered and burnt their way through the surrounding townships did not do so purely at the behest of Buthelezi and his lieutenants. Ideas of Zulu ethnicity were simply not that strong, without the reinforcement of the urban distinctions between insiders and outsiders, and the consequent socio-economic, and thus political, bifurcation of those who had come to live in the towns, however temporarily.

The ANC was by no means an innocent victim of these attacks, even though they attempted, with considerable success, to portray themselves as such. Out of pure belligerence, and initial mistrust of a man they were not yet confident would not sell out their interests, the Natal ANC, with widespread support, refused to allow Mandela to work his personal magic on Buthelezi immediately after his release. They thus cut off an option which might have shortened the war, and saved hundreds of lives. When its supporters had the opportunity, they were as murderous as any of their opponents in the war in KwaZulu-Natal and on the Rand. In September 1992, the ANC also attempted to hasten the re-incorporation of Ciskei into the Republic by launching a mass march to its capital, Bisho. It hoped thus to unseat its dictator, Oupa Gqozo, who had been imposed by a South African-led coup a couple of years earlier. This was met by the Ciskei defence force, whose gunfire dispersed the march at the cost of twenty-nine dead. It was only by the greatest good fortune that these did not include any of the prominent ANC leaders, notably Cyril Ramaphosa, who had participated.

By this stage, Gqozo was one of a minority of Bantustan leaders who had not abandoned their privileged position under the old order to make peace with the ANC. Buthelezi and Lucas Mangope of Bophuthatswana were the others. For the rest, a coup in Venda in 1990 had delivered this area of the far north. The leaders of the other Transvaal Bantustans switched sides, entrenching their positions to the consternation of their erstwhile foes, particularly in Lebowa. Most significantly, General Bantu Holomisa, who had risen through the chaos and corruption of Transkeian politics to run this Bantustan, quickly appreciated the way in which the South African political landscape was shifting and allied with the ANC. He was even prepared to defy the South African government by offering refuge to Chris Hani, legendary MK commander and leading Communist, when the latter was temporarily banned from the Republic.

It was against the background of localised civil war that the formal negotiations ran on. The Convention for a Democratic South Africa (CODESA) met for the first time in December 1991, and over the next months seemed to be getting nowhere. Public posturing and squabbles over procedure and participation threatened to wreck it, and in May 1992 CODESA II collapsed. This was followed by the worst massacre, at Boipatong, a large, grim informal settlement to the south of Johannesburg. De Klerk had paid it a visit, in an attempt to increase his support, but his presence, together with a large police contingent, only inflamed the African residents. The police in their armoured vehicles, known as Casspirs, began to fire, and killed scores of people. Mandela blamed De Klerk, holding him personally responsible for what occurred. It seemed as though no solution could be found for South Africa's political and social divides.

In fact, the breakdown of CODESA and the Boipatong and, slightly later, Bisho massacres forced both the National Party and the ANC to realise that, come what may, a negotiated settlement had to be found. Moreover, that settlement could only be made in secret, by the leaders, over the heads of their respective supporters, and then presented as a fait accompli. This work was then performed by two young politicians, Cyril Ramaphosa for the ANC and Roelf Meyer for the government, in over forty private meetings. It is generally accepted that, to the extent that negotiations can be a contest, Ramaphosa won comprehensively. His long experience in the National Union of Mineworkers gave him skills which no one in the National Party could match, hampered as it was by half a century of unchallenged rule.

Through the complicated negotiations, three matters were at the centre. The first was the nature and powers of the body which would take over from the tricameral parliament which was still the *de jure* legislative assembly of the country. Would it merely be concerned to draft and ratify the new constitution, or would it also have legislative functions? Linked to this, there was dispute on the form of the transitional government, the place that the various parties would have in it and the period for which it would rule. To put matters crudely, the National Party hoped to string matters out for as long as possible, to maintain its own powers in government and to limit the competence of the assembly to constitution writing. The ANC in contrast wanted the elected representatives (of whom they reasonably expected to be a majority) to have as much power as possible as soon as possible. However, once the Nationalists had agreed that the constituent assembly be elected, they had in fact conceded its power to rule. What then emerged was an agreement by which for the first years after the election there would be a Government of National Unity, in which all parties which had over 5 per cent of the vote would have ministerial office, and in which a two-thirds majority would be needed to write the constitution. The assembly would have full legislative powers, subject to certain safeguards.

Secondly, there was the position of the employees of the old governments, of both South Africa and the Bantustans, in the civil service, the police and the defence forces. This was an enormous constituency, for the National Party above all. Forty per cent of employed Afrikaners worked for the government. They would have the power to wreck and to obstruct, if no longer to create. It was once again Joe Slovo who was able to find a solution, and to have it accepted. He accepted publicly the unpalatable truth that the state had not been defeated, and that it would be necessary to achieve a reconciliation with these people. Therefore, he proposed that for ten years after the transfer of government state employees would be secure in their jobs. After vigorous debate the ANC executive was prepared to accept such a proposition, while the National Party did so almost at once – a remarkable contrast for measures deriving from the country's most notorious Communist. Thereafter, the road to a settlement was open.

Thirdly, how was South Africa to be divided, and what were to be the powers of the provincial governments? In essence, the ANC, with its tradition of contacts with the old Soviet bloc, wanted to see power concentrated at the centre, while both the Inkatha Freedom Party and the National Party, that old centralistic monolith, envisaged a South Africa in which regional governments controlled wide sections of policy. It knew it could not dominate the centre, but hoped in this way to run many sectors of society, at least in some parts of the country. Eventually, the ANC came to accept that the provincial governments might have wide competence, for instance in education. The example of the Federal Republic of Germany persuaded it that provincial governments might be run by other parties than those at the centre, without there being a threat to national sovereignty. At the same time, it was realised that two of the old four provinces were far too unwieldy

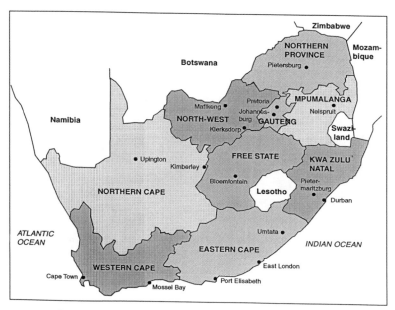

5 The New Provinces

to be effective, and South Africa was henceforth to be divided into nine provinces.

The result of these negotiations was an interim constitution agreed upon in November 1993 and adopted by the tricameral Parliament in the next month. Importantly, this meant that the transition from apartheid to democracy was achieved with constitutional continuity, something on which both Mandela and De Klerk, two lawyers of conservative temperament, always insisted. The country's laws might be changed; the supremacy of its law was maintained. A date was set for the first universal elections in South Africa's history. From 26 to 29 April 1994, South Africa would go to the polls to elect a new constituent and legislative assembly, and thereby a new president.

It had been hard enough to reach this settlement. De Klerk and the National Party finally agreed because they believed that with their contacts in the army, the civil service and the business community the country could not be run without their cooperation, and thus in effect

7.8 South African cuisine has only achieved sophistication under
Asian influences, whether produced by the slave cooks of the
Western Cape and their descendants, or by the Indians of Natal.
Elsewhere the stress has been on the circumstances in which food
is cooked, which should be out of doors. The *braaivlees*, of
spiced sausage known as *boerewors* and chops barbecued over
an open fire and accompanied by large quantities of beer and
wine, became the prime expression of suburban white society,
one to which those who were excluded on racial grounds often
aspired.

their veto. Nevertheless, it became clear that the ANC, with Mandela
at its head, was able to control much of the country. This became
evident when, on 10 April 1993, Chris Hani was assassinated in front of
his house in a once white suburb of Boksburg, where he had moved to
enjoy the sort of life-style from which he had so long been excluded (and
apparently to ensure that his children enjoyed the sort of education,
including Latin, which he himself had received). Luckily, his assassin
was quickly arrested, on the basis of information given by an Afrikaner
neighbour. Mandela appealed for calm, and was heard. Hani was
buried with full state honours, and the participation of the Catholic
bishop of Johannesburg, who argued that being the Secretary-General
of the Communist Party had not alienated Hani from the faith in which
he was brought up.

It was harder to ensure that elections throughout the country (on its boundaries as established in 1910) and the process of transition would take place in reasonable peace. For this there were three prime obstacles; Buthelezi and the Inkatha Freedom Party, Mangope and the still nominally independent Bophuthatswana, and the white right, both the halfway respectable Afrikaner nationalists associated with the army top and the Conservative Party, and the roughneck racists of the *Afrikaner Weerstandsbeweging* (AWB) under Eugene Terre'blanche.

In the frantic months leading up to April 1994, attempts to placate these various groups were mutually contradictory. The ANC entered into negotiations with General Constand Viljoen, the revered former head of the South African Defence Force, for the establishment of a *volkstaat*, in which Afrikaans religion, culture and language would be preserved. The difficulty was the practical one of finding an area in which Afrikaners were in a majority. There was none, and Ramaphosa once suggested Robben Island as the only possibility. All the same, the goodwill shown seemed to be bringing much of the right into the discussions. These broke down when contrasted with the hard line which the ANC was taking with Buthelezi. Since Buthelezi was likely to become premier of KwaZulu-Natal, one of the new provinces (which in this case was a continuation of the old one), the ANC was attempting to diminish the power of regional governments vis-à-vis the centre.

The result was that Viljoen decided to move into Bophuthatswana with 4,000 troops. Nominally, this was to preserve the independence of an ally; in fact, it gave him the opportunity of establishing a base, into which the army might move much of its equipment, from which to challenge the new government. However, his reasonably disciplined forces were joined, against his wishes, by a rabble from the AWB. Their actions, shooting blacks for the fun of it, led to a mutiny of the Bophuthatswana army. Three men, the last in the convoy, were caught as their car broke down, and were executed by a Bophuthatswana colonel in full view of the television cameras. That symbol of the new balance of forces closed off Viljoen's options. Almost immediately he agreed to participate in the elections, leading a party known as the Freedom Front, as the best way of achieving his objectives.

Buthelezi held out to the last possible moment, but in the end, under considerable international pressure, he too agreed to participate in the elections. How far he had been bluffing it is difficult to say; certainly in the end he made the only decision that could prevent his political base in KwaZulu being overrun by the army of the new South Africa. The ballot papers had already been printed, but in a great hurry many millions of stickers were manufactured to be attached to those papers to allow the new South African electorate to vote for the Inkatha Freedom Party.

Between 26 and 29 April 1994, 19,726,610 South Africans voted in the founding election of the new South Africa. At least, that many had their votes counted. There were no violent incidents on the polling days.

For most of them, voting was a liberating, a cathartic, almost a religious, experience. Long lines stretched back from the polling stations, but the people remained quiet in the sun. Once they had entered the polling booth, they celebrated the new order, or partially relieved themselves of their guilt, by the single, private ritual of putting a cross on a piece of paper, folding it up and depositing it through the slit of a locked box.

In many parts of the country, the organisation of the election was a shambles. The structures of local government were neither all-pervasive nor impartial enough to be trusted with the election. Local businessmen and others were brought in to form an ad hoc electoral commission. Generally, they did well, but in a minority of places matters failed, as might be expected given the time they had had for preparation and training. The police and the defence force solved numerous logistical problems, as if purging themselves of their history in preventing the emergence of South Africa's democracy. The Air Force flew 600 tons of ballot papers from Europe, and during the election itself made 175 special missions, to facilitate what it had once tried to prevent.

In many areas, notably the Western Cape, everything went smoothly. In others, local powers did all they could to ensure that the result was as they wanted it. There were many allegations of ballot boxes being stuffed, or disappearing. The count was chaotic and disputed. In the end, in KwaZulu-Natal and elsewhere, the result was determined by negotiation. A clause had been inserted into the electoral legislation which laid down, broadly translated, that if the parties in question were agreed on what the result should be, then the Electoral Commission would declare that to have been the result.

7.9 Queuing to vote in Guguletu, Cape Town, 27 April 1994.

For all its imperfections as a perfect democratic exercise, the election provided a reasonably accurate representation of opinion of all South Africans, although in some ways too good to be true. The ANC won 62.65 per cent of the vote, a substantial majority, but not enough to allow it to write the constitution on its own, and captured seven of the nine provinces. Outside of Natal it received very wide support from Africans of all class and ethnic backgrounds. Its Sotho support was as large as its Xhosa one, and its middle-class support as high as that among the poor. Only in the industrial heartland of the southern Transvaal, now renamed Gauteng province,* are there indications that some Africans voted against the ANC on a class basis. Even there in general, and certainly elsewhere, the richer voted for the ANC, either out of solidarity and gratitude as Africans or because they felt that an ANC government would increase their prosperity, as well as that of the poorer Africans.

With just under half the votes in the official count, Inkatha took control of KwaZulu-Natal, and had 10.54 per cent of the national total. Seven-eighths of its votes were in that single province, over which Buthelezi would become premier.

---

* The place of gold, in Setswana.

7.10 The inauguration of President Nelson Mandela and Vice-president Thabo Mbeki.

The National Party received 20.04 per cent of the vote across the country, just above a psychological barrier and one which allowed it to nominate De Klerk as one of the vice-presidents. It did however manage a clear majority in the single province of the Western Cape. In addition to its white support, as elsewhere, it also took about two-thirds of the coloured vote in the region. Relatively speaking, the ANC did better amongst the more educated, and thus more politicised, coloureds, and where it could exploit its connection with COSATU, but lost heavily in the countryside. Fear of the ANC as godless and violent, distrust of its candidate for premier, the publicly adulterous dominee Allan Boesak, worries about jobs in groups which had been relatively privileged by the Coloured Labour Preference policy, and habits of deference all played their part in this.

In a sense, these aberrancies from the national pattern were irrelevant. On 10 May 1994, F.W. de Klerk and Thabo Mbeki were sworn in as the two vice-presidents of a united country. Then Nelson Mandela took the oath as the first president of a country in which the scars of the past were temporarily hidden, before a vast and jubilant multitude. Six jets of the South African air force saluted him, trailing smoke in the colours of the new South African flag in which the red, white and blue of the old flag were allied with the black, green and gold of the ANC.

Just before the fly-past, Nelson Mandela ended his inauguration speech with the words: 'Let freedom reign. God bless Africa.' I do not believe that he was aware of the pun. Nevertheless, it was culturally totally appropriate.

8

Epilogue: the acid rain of freedom

There are fairly short limits to the length of time that a country can live on euphoria, even one as great as that South Africa experienced in 1994. To some extent, the structural problems of the country's society and economy had been masked by its political conflicts. The change of government brought them out into the open.

The Government of National Unity formed in 1994 included ministers from both Inkatha and the National Party as well as the ANC, as the agreement preceding the election had stipulated. In fact, the ANC came to dominate almost to the point of exclusivity. De Klerk had hoped that he could impose himself and the National Party as the sluice through which contacts between the ANC and the business world, the armed forces, even the civil service, had to pass. However, these groups judged that they had no need of the National Party, which was left without a role to play. After two years, it withdrew from the government, claiming that in this way it could better form the democratic opposition which the country needed, although actually it seemed to be self-destructing in internal strife.

In these circumstances, the task of delivering benefits from the political transformation was entirely in the hands of the ANC. It was not going to be easy. An attempt, on Mandela's personal initiative, to allow children to learn without the pangs of hunger by providing them with two slices of bread and peanut butter a day, worked in some areas, but also gave the opportunity for corruption. The Reconstruction and Development Programme which attempted to redress the socio-economic effects of apartheid did not have the cash to make more than a marginal difference. Indeed, the budget for 1997 was financially more stringent than anything the pre-1990 government would have dared. There were too many examples elsewhere in Africa (and indeed in the rest of the world) of the long-term debt problems caused by short-term investments with money that governments did not have for South Africa to take this route.

The legacy of apartheid was harsh, and its effects were becoming noticeable to those who had previously been cushioned from its impact. All public schools were opened to blacks, of course, which brought their deficiencies and overcrowding out of the townships into the suburbs. The crime rate probably did not increase much, but now all South Africans, and all foreign visitors, were confronted with the violence which the majority had long suffered. Johannesburg and Cape Town remained two of the most crime-ridden and unsafe places in the world, but this was now evident to those who had chosen, and had been allowed, not to see it.

All the same, by 1997 the signs were that the long slow cure of South Africa's problems had begun. A constitution of considerable liberality had been adopted. Mandela's enormous personal charm, evident absolute integrity and appreciation of the need to reconcile whites with a black-run government, if only to ensure that the benefits of their skills were distributed throughout the country, had their desired effect. In this he was aided greatly by the country's sporting success. Victory in the Rugby World Cup and in the African Nations Cup at soccer, with Mandela publicly present on both occasions as the most obviously fervent supporter, was symbolically of great importance. It was murmured that reconciliation with the former oppressors was at the cost of rewards for their victims, but Mandela's prestige seemed able to quell such matters. On the other hand, the Truth and Reconciliation Commission, chaired by Archbishop Tutu, confessor to the nation, provided intangible but genuine satisfaction. The terms were that all stories could be told and amnesty would be granted to those who admitted to human rights violations – in other words murder and assault – before 10 May 1997, a time-period which was later extended considerably. It was of real importance to the victims and their relatives that their testimony could be heard in public, and also to see some at least of the former rulers doing penance for their actions.

South Africa still has to reckon with its history. It is simply too nearly

8.1 Final of the African Nations Cup. Like Rugby, soccer was
introduced into South Africa through the mission schools, and
also through the British Army, particularly in the Western Cape
during the Boer War. Unlike Rugby, however, it spread
throughout the country, and became firmly anchored in the
townships of Gauteng. There, by the 1950s, a black professional
league had emerged, with as leading teams, the Soweto clubs,
Orlando Pirates (or 'Bucs'), Moroka Swallows (the 'Birds' whose
name derives ultimately from the badge of the London
Missionary Society) and, later, Kaiser Chiefs. There also existed
a white league and, probably because of the quality of the black
players, soccer became the first major sport to break with
apartheid divisions. It became the largest participatory and
spectator sport in the country, and the Soweto stadium was built
to hold 90,000 people. Only after 1990 were South Africans able
to measure themselves against international competition. By
1996, however, the country was strong enough to win the African
Nations Cup, which indeed it hosted, and then qualified for the
first time for the finals of the 1998 World Cup.

omnipresent for anyone to believe that in May 1994 the world had
begun afresh, as if Nongqawuse's prophecy had come true a century
and a half too late. The divisions and malformations of apartheid, the
racism still of some whites (though remarkably hardly any blacks), the
sexism of both white and black males were all too obvious, and came

out of the past. Memories could not be cleared, and psyches had been scarred.

South Africa will never be a normal country. It is far too interesting, far too rich, in its people if not in its wealth, for that. However, it is beginning to behave like one. The structures of local and provincial government, which in the end will be responsible for the delivery of services, have had to be built up anew, and are only just beginning to function. The civil war in KwaZulu-Natal is in partial remission, and is perhaps on the way to being cured. The government is pursuing a foreign policy as befits the hegemonic power in Southern Africa, and in ways which are similar in kind, if not in detail, to those of its predecessor. It tries to impose its values on surrounding states, notably Lesotho and Swaziland, and to a degree in Congo-Kinshasa. At the same time, it does what it can to make the continent beyond the boundaries of the Republic safe for the activities of South African mining companies, and commercial interests generally. The economy is growing again, at more than the rate of population growth. It will be a long time before the inequalities of the past are removed, if that ever happens. Even without this, the benefits of the new order are only very slowly reaching those who need them, and this slowness causes considerable frustration. All the same, the rain may be tainted with the past, but it is still falling. That, for most South Africans, is what matters.

SUGGESTIONS FOR
FURTHER READING

This list is a personal and partial selection of books written, or at least pub-lished, in English. It thus excludes both the extensive historical literature in Afrikaans – admittedly too often parochial and turgid – and also articles in journals, although much of the most interesting recent work has appeared in the *Journal of Southern African Studies*, the *Journal of African History* and, latterly, the *South African Historical Journal*, and also scattered through other academic journals. In addition, there have been numerous multi-author collec-tions of essays, more or less tightly organised around a theme. I also find the *Southern African Review of Books* and *The Weekly Mail and Guardian*, and also the annuals, *The South African Review* and the *Survey of Race Relations* (now the *South African Survey*) of the South African Instututute of Race Relations, essential reading.

GENERAL

De Kiewiet, *A History of South Africa, Social and Economic*, London, Oxford University Press, 1941 (old, outdated, often mistaken, and unsurpassed).

Wilson, Monica and Thompson, Leonard (eds.), *The Oxford History of South Africa*, 2 vols., Oxford, Clarendon Press, 1968–71.

Davenport, T.R.H., *South Africa: A Modern History*, London, Macmillan, 1977 (and subsequent editions).

Thompson, Leonard, *A History of South Africa*, New Haven and London, Yale University Press, 1994.

Beinart, William, *Twentieth-Century South Africa*, Oxford, Oxford University Press, 1994.

Worden, Nigel, *The Making of Modern South Africa: Conquest, Segregation and Apartheid*, Oxford, Blackwell, 1994.

Frederickson, George M., *White Supremacy: A Comparative Study in*

American and South African History, New York and Oxford, Oxford University Press, 1981.

THEMATIC, WITH A LONGER TIME SPAN

Beinart, William and Peter Coates, *Environment and History: The Taming of Nature in the USA and South Africa*, London and New York, Routledge, 1995.

Bredekamp, Henry and Robert Ross (eds.), *Missions and Christianity in South African History*, Johannesburg, Witwatersrand University Press, 1995.

Elphick, Richard and Rodney Davenport (eds.), *Christianity in South Africa: A Political, Social and Cultural History*, Oxford, James Currey, Cape Town, David Philip, Berkeley and Los Angeles, University of California Press, 1997.

Sundkler, Bengt, *Bantu Prophets in South Africa*, 2nd edition, London, Oxford University Press, 1961.

Sundkler, Bengt, *Zulu Zion and Some Swazi Zionists*, Oxford, Oxford University Press, 1976.

Duminy, Andrew and Bill Guest (eds.), *Natal and Zululand from Earliest Times to 1910: A New History*, Pietermaritzburg, University of Natal Press, 1989.

Bozzoli, Belinda (ed.), *Town and Countryside in the Transvaal: Capitalist Penetration and Popular Response*, Johannesburg, Ravan Press, 1983.

Marks, Shula, *Divided Sisterhood: Race, Class and Gender in the South African Nursing Profession*, Houndmills and London, Macmillan, 1994.

Cush, Jonathan and Charles Ambler (eds.), *Liquor and Labor in Southern Africa*, Athens, Ohio University Press and Pietermaritzburg, University of Natal Press, 1992.

Freund, Bill, *Insiders and Outsiders: The Indian Working Class in Durban*, London, James Currey, 1995.

Lewis, Gavin, *Between the Wire and the Wall: A History of South African 'Coloured' Politics*, Cape Town and Johannesburg, David Philip, 1987.

Packard, Randall M., *White Plague, Black Labor: Tuberculosis and the Political Economy of Health and Disease in South Africa*, Pietermaritzburg, University of Natal Press, 1990.

Walker, Cherryl, *Women and Resistance in South Africa*, London, Onyx Press, 1982.

Walker, Cherryl (ed.), *Women and Gender in Southern Africa to 1945*, Cape Town, David Philip, 1990.

PRE-COLONIAL SOUTH AFRICA

Hall, Martin, *The Changing Past: Farmers, Kings and Traders in Southern Africa, 200–1860*, Cape Town, David Philip, 1987.

COLONIAL SOUTH AFRICA

Elphick, Richard and Hermann Giliomee, *The Shaping of South African Society, 1652–1840*, 2nd edition, Cape Town, Maskew Miller Longman, 1989.

Shell, Robert C.-H., *Children of Bondage: A Social History of the Slave Society at the Cape of Good Hope*, Hanover and London, Wesleyan University Press, 1995.

Worden, Nigel, *Slavery in Dutch South Africa*, Cambridge, Cambridge University Press, 1985.

Ross, Robert, *Cape of Torments: Slavery and Resistance in South Africa*, London, Routledge & Kegan Paul, 1982.

Crais, Clifton C., *White Supremacy and Black Resistance in Pre-Industrial South Africa: The Making of the Colonial Order in the Eastern Cape, 1770–1865*, Cambridge, Cambridge University Press, 1992.

Mostert, Noël, *Frontiers: The Epic of South Africa's Creation and the Tragedy of the Xhosa People*, London, Jonathan Cape, 1992.

Keegan, Timothy, *Colonial Soputh Africa and the Origins of the Racial Order*, Cape Town and Johannesburg, David Philip, 1996.

Worden, Nigel and Clifton Crais (eds.), *Breaking the Chains: Slavery and its Legacy in the Nineteenth Century Cape Colony*, Johannesburg, Witwatersrand University Press, 1994.

Eldredge, Elizabeth A., *A South African Kingdom: The Pursuit of Security in Nineteenth-Century Lesotho*, Cambridge, Cambridge University Press, 1993.

Hamilton, Carolyn (ed.), *The Mfecane Aftermath: Reconstructive Debates in Southern African History*, Johannesburg and Pietermaritzburg, Witwatersrand University Press and University of Natal Press, 1995.

Delius, Peter, *The Land Belongs to Us: The Pedi Polity, the Boers and the British in the Nineteenth-Century Transvaal*, Johannesburg, Ravan Press, 1983.

Marks, Shula and Anthony Atmore (eds.), *Economy and Society in Pre-Industrial South Africa*, London, Longman, 1980.

BIOGRAPHIES

Sanders, Peter, *Moshoeshoe: Chief of the Sotho*, London, Heinemann, 1975.

Thompson, Leonard, *Survival in Two Worlds: Moshoeshoe of Lesotho, 1786–1870*, Oxford, Clarendon Press, 1975.

Van Onselen, Charles, *The Seed is Mine; the Life of Kas Maine, a South African Sharecropper, 1894–1985*, Cape Town, David Philip, 1986.

Parsons, Neil, Thomas Tlou and Willie Henderson, *Seretse Khama, 1921–1980*, Gaborone, The Botswana Society, 1995.

Couzens, Tim, *The New African: A Study of the Life and Work of H.I.E. Dhlomo*, Johannesburg, Ravan Press, 1985.

ETHNOGRAPHIES AND ANTHROPOLOGY

Hunter, Monica, *Reaction to Conquest: Effects of Contact with Europeans on the Pondo of South Africa*, London, Oxford University Press, 1935.

Krige, E.J. and J.D. Krige, *The Realm of the Rain Queen: A Study of the Pattern of Lovedu Society*, Oxford, Oxford University Press of the International African Institute, 1943.

Barnard. Alan, *Hunters and Herders of Southern Africa: A Comparative Ethnography of the Khoisan Peoples*, Cambridge, Cambridge University Press, 1992.

Kuper, Adam, *Wives for Cattle: Bridewealth and Marriage in Southern Africa*, London, Routledge & Kegan Paul, 1982.

1870–1920

Thompson, Leonard, *The Unification of South Africa, 1902–1910*, Oxford, Clarendon Press, 1960.

Worger, William H., *South Africa's City of Diamonds: Mine Workers and Monopoly Capitalism in Kimberley, 1867–1895*, New Haven and London, Yale University Press, 1987.

Turrell, Robert Vicat, *Capital and Labour on the Kimberley Diamond Mines, 1871–1890*, Cambridge, Cambridge University Press, 1987.

Van Onselen, Charles, *Studies in the Social and Economic History of the Witwatersrand, 1886–1914: Volume I, New Babylon*; Volume II, *New Nineveh*, London, Longman, 1982.

Guy, Jeff, *The Destruction of the Zulu Kingdom: The Civil War in Zululand, 1879–1884*, London, Longman, 1979.

Bonner, Philip, *Kings, Commoners and Concessionaries: The Evolution and Dissolution of the Nineteenth-Century Swazi State*, Cambridge, Cambridge University Press, 1987.

Marks, Shula, *Reluctant Rebellion: The 1906–8 Disturbances in Natal*, Oxford, Clarendon Press, 1970.

Pakenham, Thomas, *The Boer War*, Weidenfeld & Nicholson, 1979.

Marks, Shula and Richard Rathbone (eds.), *Industrialisation and Social Change in South Africa: African Class Formation, Culture and Consciousness, 1870–1930*, London, Longman, 1982.

Bundy, Colin, *The Rise and Fall of the South African Peasantry*, London, Heinemann, 1979.

Beinart, William, *The Political Economy of Pondoland, 1860–1930*, Cambridge, Cambridge University Press, 1982.

Atkins, Keletso, *The Moon is Dead! Give Us Our Money!: The Cultural Origins of an African Work Ethic, Natal, South Africa, 1843–1900*, London, James Currey, 1993.

Shillington, Kevin, *The Colonisation of the Southern Tswana, 1870–1900*, Johannesburg, Ravan Press, 1985.

Keegan, Timothy J., *Rural Transformations in Industrialising South Africa: The Southern Highveld to 1914*, Johannesburg, Ravan Press, 1986.

Harries, Patrick, *Work, Culture and Identity: Migrant Labourers in Mozambique and South Africa, c. 1860–1910*, Johannesburg, Witwatersrand University Press, 1994.

De Kiewiet, Cornelis W., *The Imperial Factory in South Africa: A Study in Politics and Economics*, Cambridge, Cambridge University Press, 1937.

Krikler, Jeremy, *Revolution from Above, Rebellion from Below: The Agrarian Transvaal at the Turn of the Century*, Oxford, Clarendon Press, 1993.

Campbell, James T., *Songs of Zion: The African Methodist Episcopal Church in the United States and South Africa*, New York and Oxford, Oxford University Press, 1995.

Smith, Iain, *The Origins of the South African War, 1899–1902*, London and New York, Longman, 1996.

Nasson, Bill, *Abraham Esau's War: A Black South African War in the Cape, 1899–1902*, Cambridge, Cambridge University Press, 1991.

Beinart, William and Colin Bundy, *Hidden Struggles in Rural South Africa: Politics and Popular Movements in the Transkei and Eastern Cape, 1890–1930*, London, James Currey, 1987.

1920–1980

Lewis, Jon, *Industrialisation and Trade Union Organisation in South Africa, 1924–1955: The Rise and Fall of the South African Trades and Labour Council*, Cambridge, Cambridge University Press, 1984.

Delius, Peter, *A Lion among the Cattle: Reconstruction and Resistance in the Northern Transvaal*, Johannesburg, Ravan Press, 1996.

Bradford, Helen, *A Taste of Freedom: The ICU in Rural South Africa, 1924–1930*, Johannesburg, Ravan Press, 1987.

Bonner, Philip, Peter Delius and Deborah Posel, *Apartheid's Genesis, 1935–1962*, Johannesburg, Ravan and Witwatersrand University Press, 1993.

Landau, Paul, *The Realm of the Word: Language, Gender and Christianity in a Southern African Kingdom*, Cape Town, David Philip, 1995.

Lodge, Tom, *Black Politics in South Africa since 1945*, London and New York, Longman, 1993.

Frederickson, George, M., *Black Liberation: A Comparative History of Black Ideologies in the United States and South Africa*, New York and Oxford, Oxford University Press, 1995.

Berger, Iris, *Threads of Solidarity: Women in South African Industry, 1900–1980*, London, James Currey, 1992.

O'Meara, Dan, *Volkscapitalism: Class, Capital and Ideology in the Development of Afrikaner Nationalism, 1934–1948*, Cambridge, Cambridge University Press, 1983.

O'Meara, Dan, *Forty Lost Years; The Apartheid State and the Politics of the National Party, 1948–1994*, Johannesburg, Ravan, 1995.

Posel, Deborah, *The Making of Apartheid, 1948–1961: Conflict and Compromise*, Oxford, Clarendon Press, 1991.

Murray, Colin, *Black Mountain: Land and Class and Power in the Eastern Orange Free State, 1880s–1980s*, Edinburgh, Edinburgh University Press, 1992.

Murray, Colin, *Families Divided: The Impact of Migrant Labour in Lesotho*, Cambridge, Cambridge University Press, 1981.

Marks, Shula and Stanley Trapido (eds.), *The Politics of Race, Class and Nationalism in Twentieth Century South Africa*, London, Longmans, 1987.

Moodie, T. Dunbar, *The Rise of Afrikanerdom: Power, Apartheid and Afrikaner Civil Religion*, Berkeley, Los Angeles and London, University of California Press, 1975.

Walshe, Peter, *The Rise of Nationalism in South Africa: The African National Congress, 1912–1952*, London, Hurst, 1970.

Dubow, Saul, *Racial Segregation and the Origins of Apartheid in South Africa, 1919–1936*, London, Macmillan, 1989.

Lipton, Merle, *Capitalism and Apartheid*, Aldershot, Macmillan, 1985.

Jones, Stuart and André Müller, *The South African Economy, 1910–90*, London, Macmillan, 1992.

Crush, Jonathan, Alan Jeeves and David Yudelman, *South Africa's Labor Empire: A History of Black Migrancy to the Gold Mines*, Boulder, San Francisco and Oxford, Westview Press and Cape Town, David Philip, 1991.

Wilson, Francis, *Labour in the South African Gold Mines, 1911–1969*, Cambridge, Cambridge University Press, 1972.

Moodie, T. Dunbar with Vivienne Ndatshe, *Going for Gold: Men, Mines and Migrancy*, Johannesburg, Witwatersrand University Press, 1994.

POST-1980

De Wet, Chris, *Moving Together, Drifting Apart: Betterment Planning and Villagisation in a South African Homeland*, Johannesburg, Witwatersrand University Press, 1995.

Wilson, Francis and Mamphela Ramphele, *Uprooting Poverty: The South African Challenge*, Cape Town and Johannesburg, David Philip, 1989.

Johnson, R.W. and Schlemmer, Lawrence, *Launching Democracy in South Africa: The First Open Election, April 1994*, New Haven and London, Yale University Press, 1996.

Van Kessel, Ineke, *'Beyond Our Wildest Dreams': The United Democratic Front and the Transformation of South Africa*, Leiden, Afrika-Studiecentrum, 1995.

Murray, Martin, *The Revolution Deferred: The Painful Birth of Post-Apartheid South Africa*, London and New York, Verso, 1994.

Marx, Anthony W., *Lessons of Struggle: South African Internal Opposition, 1960–1990*, New York and Oxford, Oxford University Press, 1992.

Mbeki, Govan, *Sunset At Midday: Lastshon'ilang'emini!*, Braamfontein, Nolwazi, 1996.

Waldmeir, Patti, *Anatomy of a Miracle: The End of Apartheid and the Birth of a New South Africa*, New York, W.W. Norton, 1997.

CULTURE

Coplan, David, *In Township Tonight! South Africa's Black City Music and Theatre*, London, Longmans, 1985.

Coplan, David, *In the Time of Cannibals: The Word Music of South Africa's Basotho Migrants*, Chicago and London, University of Chicago Press, 1994.

Erlmann, Veit, *African Stars: Studies in Black South African Performance*, Chicago, University of Chicago Press, 1991.

Erlmann, Veit, *Nightstars: Performance, Power and Practice in South Africa*, Chicago, University of Chicago Press, 1996.

Hofmeyr, Isobel, *'We Spend Our Years as a Tale that is Told': Oral Historical Narrative in a South African Chiefdom*, Johannesburg, Witwatersrand University Press, 1993.

Nixon, Rob, *Homelands, Harlem and Hollywood: South African Culture and the World Beyond*, New York and London, Routledge, 1994.

Nettleton, Anitra and David Hammond-Tooke, *African Art in Southern Africa: From Tradition to Township*, Johannesburg, Ad. Donker, 1990.

Grundlingh, Albert, André Odendaal and Burridge Spies, *Beyond the Tryline: Rugby and South African Society*, Johannesburg, Ravan, 1995.

Ballantine, Christopher, *Marabi Nights: Early South African Jazz and Vaudeville*, Johannesburg, Ravan, 1993.

MEMOIRS AND AUTOBIOGRAPHIES (A VERY PERSONAL SHORT SELECTION)

Mattera, Don, *Gone with the Twilight: A Story of Sophiatown*, London, Zed Books, 1987.

Kuzwayo, Ellen, *Call Me Woman*, London, The Woman's Press, 1985.

Malan, Rian, *My Traitor's Heart*, London, The Bodley Head, 1990.

Ramphele, Mamphela, *My Life*, Cape Town, David Philip, 1995.

Mandela, Nelson, *Long Walk to Freedom: The Autobiography of Nelson Mandela*, London, Little Brown & Company, 1994.

Mphahlele, Ezekiel, *Down Second Avenue*, Berlin, Seven Seas, 1959.

INDEX